Blood-Red the Roses

THE WARS OF THE ROSES

For thirty-five years, the Houses of York and Lancaster engaged in a bloody struggle for the throne of England. Among the fascinating and complex figures who played major roles in this incredible drama were the half-mad King Henry VI and his iron-willed wife, Queen Margaret; the proud and brilliant Richard Neville, Earl of Warwick; King Edward IV; the two young princes mysteriously murdered in the Tower of London; and the treacherous Henry Stafford, Duke of Buckingham. The years of strife between the white rose of York and the red rose of Lancaster ended on August 22, 1485, at Bosworth Field, when the army of King Richard III met the rebel forces of Henry Tudor in one of history's most decisive battles. Before the sun had set on that hot and bloody day, Richard lay dead, and England had a new ruler to lead her into an era of power and glory.

Blood-Red the Roses

THE WARS OF THE ROSES

by

CLIFFORD LINDSEY ALDERMAN

map & photographs

BAILEY BROTHERS AND SWINFEN LTD
Folkestone

Published by Bailey Brothers and Swinfen Ltd
1973

Copyright, ©, 1971 by Clifford Lindsey Alderman

SBN 561 00172 3

For our good English friends Nita and
Sid Braker, who live near Bosworth Field in
Oadby, Leicestershire

Printed in Great Britain by
Whitstable Litho, Straker Brothers Ltd

Contents

CHIEF CHARACTERS OF THE WARS OF THE ROSES

Name	Title	Side Supported	Fate
Henry of Lancaster	King Henry VI of England	Lancaster	Died, 1471, mysteriously
Margaret of Anjou, wife of Henry VI	Queen of England, Dowager Queen after death of Henry VI	Lancaster	Died, 1482, in France
Richard of York	Third Duke of York	York	Killed, battle of Wakefield, 1460
Richard Neville	Earl of Warwick (the King-maker)	York, then Lancaster	Killed, battle of Barnet, 1471
Edward, first son of Richard, third Duke of York	Earl of March, then King Edward IV of England	York	Died, 1483
George, second son of Richard, third Duke of York	Duke of Clarence	York, then Lancaster, finally York	Executed, 1478
Richard, third son of Richard, third Duke of York	Duke of Gloucester, then King Richard III of England	York	Killed at Bosworth Field, 1485
Elizabeth Woodville, wife of Edward IV	Queen of England, then Dowager Queen after death of Edward IV	York (no part in fighting)	Died, imprisoned, 1492
Edward, first son of Edward IV	Prince of Wales, then King Edward V of England, never crowned	York (no part in fighting)	Vanished, supposedly murdered, probably in 1483
Richard, second son of Edward IV	Duke of York	York (no part in fighting)	Vanished, supposedly murdered, probably in 1483
Edward, son of Henry VI	Prince of Wales	Lancaster	Killed, battle of Tewkesbury, 1471
Henry Tudor	Henry VII, first Tudor King of England	Lancaster	Died, 1509

PRINCIPAL BATTLES OF THE WARS OF THE ROSES

Battle	Date	Lancastrian Commander	Yorkist Commander	Winner
First St. Albans	May 22, 1455	Edmund Beaufort, 2nd Duke of Somerset	Richard, Duke of York	York
Blore Heath	Sept. 23, 1459	James Toucher, Lord Audley	Earl of Salisbury	York
Northampton	July 10, 1460	Humphrey Stafford, 1st Duke of Buckingham	Richard Neville, Earl of Warwick	York
Wakefield	Dec. 30, 1460	Margaret of Anjou (actual, probably Andrew Trollope)	Richard, Duke of York	Lancaster
Mortimer's Cross	Feb. 2, 1461	Earls of Pembroke and Wiltshire	King Edward IV	York
Second St. Albans	Feb. 17, 1461	Margaret of Anjou	Richard Neville, Earl of Warwick	Lancaster
Towton	March 29, 1461	Henry Percy, Earl of Northumberland	King Edward IV	York
Hexham	May 14, 1464	Henry Beaufort, 3rd Duke of Somerset	John Neville, Marquess of Montagu	York
Banbury	July 26, 1469	Robin of Redesdale	Earl of Pembroke	Lancaster
Stamford	March 12, 1470	Sir Robert Welles	King Edward IV	York
Barnet	April 14, 1471	Richard Neville, Earl of Warwick	King Edward IV	York
Tewkesbury	May 4, 1471	Edmund Beaufort, 4th Duke of Somerset	King Edward IV	York
Bosworth Field	Aug. 22, 1485	Henry Tudor	King Richard III	Lancaster

I

The Strange First Battle
of St. Albans

In May, 1455, an armed body of about a thousand men marched out of Warwick Castle in the Midlands, the very heart of England. No more colourful force can be imagined than this one. The men wore red jackets or surcoats emblazoned with the Ragged Staff emblem—or livery, as it was called—of Richard Neville, Earl of Warwick.

It was probably the most famous insignia of war in all England. If you cut off the top of a Christmas tree, stripped it of its needles and twigs, and lopped off the branches so that only stubs remained sticking out along the main stem, you would have something much like the Ragged Staff.

The leader of this force, mounted on a splendid charger, was no less striking than his men. The only portrait known that is said to be his shows him with a long, narrow, triangular face, a hard mouth and stern, arrogant eyes. He was tall, lean and powerfully built. At the head of his army, wearing his visored helmet with a sable plume on its crest, he looked even taller. Under his short, loose coat he wore a steel breastplate inlaid with gold that was polished until it shone like the sun. He was

9

an awesome figure, this man, Richard Neville, Earl of Warwick.

And indeed Warwick, as he is usually called, towered in
other ways over the leading men of his time. He had won victories in war, was one of the richest men in England and had
achieved great success as a statesman and diplomat. Above all,
he had a magnetism that drew men to him, ready to follow
the Ragged Staff livery anywhere.

Since Richard Neville, Earl of Warwick, was one of the most
important figures of the ·Wars of the Roses, which tore England, off and on, for thirty years from 1455 to 1485, it is well
to know something of his history. He was born November 27,
1428, the eldest son of the Earl of Salisbury, also named Richard Neville, in Yorkshire, probably at one of his father's castles
there, Middleham.

Violence was a keynote of life in England in the fifteenth
century, and as a boy Richard Neville learned that a nobleman
had to live violently in order to survive. This was especially
true in the northern region of England where he was brought
up. Wild country it was, a land of desolate moors and crags,
its inhabitants wild people, all but impossible to control.

Young Richard Neville probably began his training in riding
and the use of arms at an early age, along with his younger
brothers. Probably, too, as soon as he was old enough, he was
with his father when the elder Neville and his retainers—the
fighting men he maintained at the castle—went forth to keep
peace in the countryside. There were raids by the even wilder
Scots from across the border to the north and raids by bands
of robbers, outlaws and murderers who stole sheep and ravaged
and burned villages.

The younger Richard came by his title of Earl of Warwick

through his marriage. Naturally, as was the custom among English nobility, it had already been arranged when Richard was only ten years old. But a more fortunate one can scarcely be imagined.

It did not seem so at first, even though it would bring a considerable fortune to young Richard. His bride, Anne Beauchamp, daughter of Richard Beauchamp, then the thirteenth Earl of Warwick, had a younger brother who inherited his father's title and vast land holdings when the earl died in 1439. But in 1447 the brother also died suddenly. Since this left Anne as the heiress, Richard Neville, her husband, became Earl of Warwick. He also became lord of more than fifty estates with their manors, castles and privileges all over England—in the shires of Warwick, Oxford, Hertford, Suffolk, Essex, Hampshire, Berkshire, Wiltshire, Devonshire, Cornwall and Durham. Thus Richard Neville, the new Earl of Warwick, had wealth, high rank and the power that went with them.

Now, in 1455, Warwick marched eastward with his army across the Midlands. They reached Ermine Street, or the Great North Road, one of the system of long highways out of London built by the Romans from the first to the fifth centuries. There they met Richard, Duke of York, and Warwick's father, the Earl of Salisbury, with their armies.

The strength of their combined forces is estimated at about 3,000 men. There were archers, some afoot, some mounted, wearing steel caps, with their leather jackets reinforced underneath with chain mail, a sword or a club of lead in their belts, their bows over their shoulders and their quivers of yard-long, steel-tipped and barbed arrows slung on their backs. There were the billmen, afoot or mounted, with their murderous bills, knights attended by their esquires and the nobles, all mounted, with both themselves and their steeds encased in heavy, cumbersome armour.

The bill, or halberd, was a frightful weapon. On the end of a long staff was mounted a broad, hook-shaped, keen-edged blade. At both the back and end of the blade were pikes, a short, pointed spear. Thus the billman could hew with his blade or stab with the pike. Even chain mail could not withstand the onslaught of the bill.

This army, commanded by Richard, Duke of York, marched straight toward London. This was the beginning of the long struggle between the houses of York and Lancaster for the throne of England.

King Henry VI of the House of Lancaster, which had ruled England more than half a century, had learned of the Yorkist advance by this time. He hastily assembled his own force and marched north out of London on May 21 for Leicester. His army was smaller than the Duke of York's—about 2,000 men— but it was led by a formidable array of great lords. Since Henry had no military talent whatsoever, the command was given to Edmund Beaufort, Duke of Somerset, the Duke of York's deadly enemy. There were also Humphrey Stafford, Duke of Buckingham; the Earls of Pembroke, Northumberland, Devon and Wiltshire; and other lords of high degree.

The King's army took another of the old Roman roads, Watling Street, running northwest from London toward Leicester. Meanwhile, York and his men were coming down the Great North Road. On the night of May 21 the Lancastrian army was about twenty miles southwest of the Yorkists. Between them lay the town of St. Albans. By that time each army knew the other's location from reports by scouts. The next morning both marched for St. Albans.

Today St. Albans is a good-sized, smart-looking market town with little resemblance to its huge neighbour, London. Yet it is very ancient, one of the oldest towns in all Britain. The invading Romans founded it as Verulamium, and some of its ruins still stand just southwest of the modern town. It also has an ancient abbey, originally built by the Saxons in honour of St. Alban, the first martyr to be put to death by the Romans for his belief in Christianity, and later rebuilt by William the Conqueror's Normans. The scene of the battle in 1455, St. Peter's Street (St. Albans' main thoroughfare) and two side streets, is still there today.

St. Albans in 1455 was not a walled town. Its only protection was a series of wooden barriers, which could be swung across the streets, and a ditch that had been dug around the town, originally surmounted by a palisade which had long since rotted away.

When the Yorkist army approached St. Albans from the east, the Lancastrians had already occupied the opposite side of the ditch. The Yorkists halted, and Richard, Duke of York sent Humphrey Stafford, the old Duke of Buckingham, to the King's position for a parley.

The Duke of York was not then ready to strike for the throne. What he wanted most was to be rid of his enemy, the King's commander, Edmund Beaufort, Duke of Somerset. York's message, borne by Buckingham, said that the King's promises had not been kept, and that the Yorkists now demanded that "such persons as they could accuse" be delivered up to them "to have as they deserved."

The Duke of Somerset knew perfectly well that this was a demand for his own head. He took it upon himself to speak for the King, and after a long argument which came to nothing, old Buckingham went back to his camp with a refusal. Richard, Duke of York, then gave the command to attack.

The abbot of the abbey was an eyewitness of the battle, probably from the top of its great gateway, which still stands, and he wrote an account of it. From his vantage point he could look into the streets of the town and follow the action closely.

There was great alarm in St. Albans. The street barriers had been closed, and the abbey bells were pealing madly as the Yorkist army advanced toward the Lancastrian Duke of Somerset's men in their strong position across the ditch.

The Duke of York split his army into three divisions. One attacked Sopwell Lane, leading into the main street toward the south end of the town; another attempted to enter through Shropshire Lane, near the centre. The third, led by Richard, Earl of Warwick, hurled itself against the steep side of the ditch on the east.

Neither side had artillery, but the archers of both launched a torrent of arrows. Then the billmen locked in a short but desperate combat in which neither army gained much advantage, though the King's Lancastrian troops still held their ground.

Then Warwick, at the head of his red-coated troops, led them in an assault across the ditch and smashed through the Lancastrian line, breaking it in two, while the Yorkist trumpets blared triumphantly and the leader shouted: "A Warwick! A Warwick!" They got into St. Peter's Street; then half of them wheeled right and half left, putting them behind the King's Lancastrian army.

Now the rest of the Yorkist army poured through the breach in the enemy line. Although Richard, Earl of Warwick had outmaneuvered the King's troops and they were outnumbered, the Lancastrians put up a heroic struggle. The watching abbot wrote, "Here you saw one fall with his brains dashed out, there another with a broken arm, a third with a cut throat, and a fourth with a pierced chest, and the whole street was full of dead corpses."

King Henry VI, being no warrior, simply sat under a tree by the royal standard near the south end of St. Peter's Street. Then one shaft of a shower of Yorkist arrows found its mark, wounding him in the neck. A second arrow struck the Duke of Buckingham in the face. Since arrows could not usually pierce heavy armour, both men had probably lifted the protecting visors of their helmets at the time.

The Lancastrians had lost the battle. Now the Yorkists surged in upon the King. Mildly, he spoke to them: "Forsooth! Forsooth! Ye do foully to smite a king anointed so."

He was all alone. Even his standard bearer had thrown down the royal banner and fled. But the Yorkists did not harm the King. They fell to their knees and begged forgiveness, which he granted, then gently led him to the house of a tanner nearby, where his bleeding wound was staunched and bound up.

Richard, Duke of York, had not only won a battle but accomplished his great objective. Just a few yards from where the King had sat, at the corner of St. Peter's Street and Shropshire Lane (today Victoria Street), lay his great enemy, Edmund Beaufort, Duke of Somerset, dead.

Most of the other Lancastrian leaders were either killed or captured because their heavy armour kept them from escaping. The Earl of Northumberland was dead, and the Duke of Buckingham's son, the Earl of Stafford, was mortally wounded. Yet there were surprisingly few casualties among the fighting men of both armies.

It was a strange battle indeed. True, Richard, Duke of York, took advantage of his triumph by assuming the staff of the Constable of England, commander of the royal armies, the post the Duke of Somerset had held. He gave other important jobs in the government to friends and supporters, including the Earl of Salisbury and his son Richard, Earl of Warwick, the real hero of the first battle of St. Albans.

On the other hand, the Lancastrian, Henry VI, was still King and acknowledged so by Richard, Duke of York. They rode to London together, and the King was received joyfully by the people. When a new Parliament met that July, the Duke of York and all the other Yorkist leaders took a new oath of allegiance to the King and were given a royal pardon for what had happened at St. Albans. York knew the time was not yet ripe for an attempt upon the throne. And when Henry VI relieved Richard, Duke of York, of his duties as Protector, the duke made no objection.

Now, for a time, there was peace in England, but the old hatreds and ambitions still smouldered, and the death struggle between the houses of Lancaster and York was only beginning.

II

How It Began

The Wars of the Roses. No other conflict has such a charming name. It conjures up a picture of knights in shining armour, mounted on swift steeds, charging down on each other with all the colourful pageantry of the age of chivalry. One thinks of them as fighting gallantly, with loyalty and devotion, either to the White Rose of York or the Red Rose of Lancaster.

Alas, the Wars of the Roses were nothing of the kind. Even the name is false. True, the White Rose was the symbol of the House of York, but the Red Rose did not come into use until after Henry VII, first of the Tudor rulers, gained the throne. William Shakespeare is largely responsible for the mistake, since in his tragedies about these wars, *Henry the Sixth* and *Richard the Third,* he refers to the Red Rose of Lancaster. And while at least it makes them easy to remember, in this tremendously important series of wars, the roses were red—with blood.

The Wars of the Roses were brutal, vicious, bloody conflicts in which loyalty was often forgotten and treason flourished. Their principal characters included four kings (one murdered before he could be crowned), three queens and a bewildering array of dukes, duchesses, earls, countesses, knights, other noblemen and influential clergy and untitled men. There were so many, and their plots, treasons and murders so numerous, that the Wars of the Roses are probably the most difficult of all English conflicts to follow and understand. Most of the men were unprincipled ruffians, and all who took leading parts in these wars fought for one thing—power.

It was a strange conflict in many ways. For one thing, it was fought to a great extent not by the common people but by the rulers and the great dukes and earls, with the armed forces they maintained on their estates. The farmers and the working people of the towns, in general, kept out of it.

To understand why the Wars of the Roses began it is necessary to go back to the fourteenth century. In 1339 King Edward III of England invaded France. It was the beginning of the longest conflict of the Middle Ages—the Hundred Years War, that did not end until 1453, although there were periods of peace when truces were agreed upon.

At times during the Hundred Years War, great victories gave England control of most of France, but later the French began to prevail. When the Hundred Years War ended, England had lost all her vast possessions in France except for the fortress town of Calais, directly across the narrowest part of the English Channel from Dover.

The Hundred Years War had left England in a state of near-anarchy—a lawless absence of government. There was no justice—only corruption and tyranny in the courts of law. The royal ministers were untrustworthy and hated. The highways were infested with robbers, and no one dared travel then without an armed escort. And there was no real king of England.

After the death of King Henry V, in France in 1422, his two-year-old son became King Henry VI. Of course, he could not actually reign, and England was placed under the rule of a regent and a protector until the young King became of age.

An intense rivalry had sprung up at this time between two great noble families—the Nevilles and the Beauforts. The Nevilles had gained their influence through the marriage of Cicely Neville to the powerful Richard, Duke of York, who had royal blood, since he was descended from one of King Edward III's younger sons. The Beauforts also had royal blood and a claim to the throne. The Wars of the Roses developed out of a struggle between the Nevilles, representing the House of York, and the Beauforts, of the House of Lancaster.

With the baby boy, Henry VI, as another Lancastrian king, the House of York cast greedy eyes upon the throne of England. Its chances to wrest the throne away from Henry VI were good. It was during the Lancastrian rule that England lost almost all of her possessions in France. Many of the nobles were enraged, and ready for a change in the rule of England. The House of York might have been able to seize the crown quite easily but for one event—the marriage of Henry VI to Margaret of Anjou.

In 1442 young Henry reached the age of twenty-one and became King in fact as well as title. He was a weak ruler in more ways than one. Physically—though he was tall and slender and had no deformities—he had no great strength. And he was benevolent, merciful, truly pious and artless—qualities which no king in those days of brutality, cunning and treachery could have and survive unless he had powerful help.

The help came from Margaret. Since in those days royal marriages were almost always made for political reasons rather than love, Henry had to have a bride who could salvage something from the wreckage of England's former power in France. His advisers wanted to obtain a bride of the French royal family for him, but in Paris wily King Charles VII saw through the scheme. However, as a concession to good relations between France and England, he offered his niece, Margaret of Anjou.

It seemed the best match that could be obtained, though it promised little. Margaret was a princess, but she had no estates and no money in that age when a royal bride was expected to bring her husband a handsome dowry. Nevertheless, in 1445 she came to England and was married to Henry. She was only fifteen and was a most attractive girl. However, she was ambitious, arrogant and strong-willed, and she had the spirit of a tigress. Without her to advise, scheme and fight for him, poor Henry VI would almost surely have been doomed long before he was. Henry VI was held in affection by his people, but they were thoroughly disgusted with his government. It was all very well to have a king who was benevolent and merciful, but at that time especially a strong man was needed.

Then, suddenly, two events took place which stirred new turmoil. First, Henry VI became insane. Ordinarily, in such a case, a regent would be appointed to rule in the King's stead, but for a time nothing was done about it. Queen Margaret and the powerful Lancastrian, Edmund Beaufort, Duke of Somerset, governed England.

Then the second, almost unbelievable thing happened. Since Henry VI and Queen Margaret had been married nearly eight years without having children, it seemed that there was no prospect of an heir to succeed Henry on the throne. But on October 13, 1453, Queen Margaret gave birth to a son, named

Edward. The baby prince was shown to the wretched King Henry, but his disordered mind failed to recognize his son.

However, the Yorkists were so powerful that their demands for a regent could no longer be ignored. Although he was not given this title, Richard, Duke of York, was appointed Protector and Defender of the Realm, which amounted to the same thing.

But a third event changed everything once more. At Christmas, 1454, King Henry suddenly recovered. Yorkists who had been appointed to high government positions were put out of office and replaced by Lancastrians.

This was the end of the shaky truce between the houses of Lancaster and York. Richard, Duke of York, decided he had to do something to regain the hold on the government the House of York had lost. Edmund Beaufort, Duke of Somerset, and other Lancastrians were back in power, while the Yorkists had lost their influence. The duke went north, where his chief allies were, raised an army and marched for London. That was when the first battle of the Wars of the Roses took place, the first of two battles fought at St. Albans.

III

Triumph for the White Rose of York

Toward the end of 1455 King Henry's mind failed again, and once more Richard, Duke of York, was appointed Protector. But this time the King's illness was brief. By January, 1456, he was greatly improved.

Henry, gentle and forgiving soul that he was, held no grudge against the Duke of York for his rebellious attack at St. Albans. He would have been content to allow York to continue as his chief counselor, but Queen Margaret would have none of it. She wanted York arrested and tried for treason. But although she was in effect the real ruler of England, this time Henry's backbone stiffened and he refused to allow it. The Queen had to be content with seeing York removed as Protector once more and ordered back to Ireland to his former post of Lieutenant, or governor, there. But he did not go.

Richard, Earl of Warwick, was also a threat, but he had obtained the post of Captain of Calais, England's last foothold in France. While he was in command there he made himself a national hero in the eyes of the British people, thus strengthening the power of the House of York.

An attempt was made to extend into a lasting peace the truce that followed the first battle of St. Albans. A grand council, to which all the great lords were invited, was held in London. The Yorkist Dukes of York and Salisbury, Henry Beaufort, the new young Lancastrian Duke of Somerset, and many others were there. Richard, Earl of Warwick, came over from Calais.

At the start it seemed like anything but a peace conference. The streets of London swarmed with armed men, the retainers the lords kept on their estates—knights, esquires and others— who had come with them. They all seemed to be itching for a fight, and the people of the city were terrified. But at last a "reconciliation" was worked out.

On March 25, 1456, a grand procession moved through the streets of the city toward the great cathedral of St. Paul's. Close to the head of the parade marched that sad figure, King Henry VI, wearing his golden crown. Just ahead of him, hand in hand, were the new Lancastrian Duke of Somerset, Henry Beaufort, and his Yorkist enemy, the Earl of Salisbury, then Yorkist Richard Neville, Earl of Warwick, with the Lancastrian Henry Holland, Duke of Exeter. Behind the King came Queen Margaret, hand in hand with Richard, Duke of York.

It was a peaceful spectacle, all right, and the people of London, sick and tired of war, were overjoyed. But it was too good to believe, and it meant absolutely nothing. The old hatreds and rivalries were as strong as ever. Queen Margaret was still determined to have revenge upon Warwick by ousting him as Captain of Calais. She failed, and then came Warwick's great triumphs, which made him a figure even more to be feared by the House of Lancaster.

That summer of 1458 a fleet of armed Spanish merchantmen approached Calais. There were twenty-eight of them, including sixteen big forecastle ships, so called because of the towering structures on their bows. Despite his brilliant success at St. Albans, Warwick was a far better statesman than general, but his real love was the navy. He had a small one at Calais—five forecastle ships, three smaller caravels and four little sailing vessels called pinnaces.

Spain and England were not then at war. Nevertheless, piracy was rampant in the English Channel, and such a powerful fleet's approach might bode no good for Calais. Warwick did not wait to find out. Scorning the Spaniards' superiority, he took his little navy out and attacked. For six hours the battle raged, cannons thundering and each side maneuvering for the best position. Warwick's gunners damaged six enemy ships so badly that they had to surrender; one or two were sent to the bottom, and the rest turned and fled. The news of this and of raids the earl constantly made on French villages, burning and looting them, gave Warwick a reputation and popularity, especially among the men of Kent (the English shire closest to Calais), that amounted to hero worship.

That autumn of 1458 Richard, Earl of Warwick, found out how hollow the "reconciliation" was. He was summoned to England. When he and the red-jacketed guard he had brought with him entered the palace of Westminster, the servants of the royal household jeered at them. The Red Jackets were not men to be insulted by menials, and a fight began, in which Warwick loyally took part. When soldiers at the palace jumped into the fray, the earl himself had to fight for his life.

"You provoked this fight," Queen Margaret charged him haughtily. "Your resignation as Captain of Calais is demanded. You will turn over your duties to the Duke of Somerset."

"Only Parliament can withdraw my appointment," Warwick retorted.

Margaret knew better than to lay the matter before a Parliament that would never oust such a popular hero. She summoned a council of lords upon whom she could depend to turn the earl out. He told them tersely that he would not resign, and went back to Calais.

But Warwick knew there must soon be a showdown. In the summer of 1459 he received news from Richard, Duke of York, and his father, the Earl of Salisbury, in England. Queen Margaret and her supporters were assembling a powerful army to crush the Yorkists once and for all.

Warwick left Calais almost at once with six hundred of the trained garrison—four hundred archers and two hundred men-at-arms. He landed at Sandwich in Kent and marched for London. There he was joyfully received by the mayor and aldermen, while the people jammed the streets, waving their hats and shouting greetings.

The King and Queen were not there. Henry had gone north to Leicester, and Margaret and little Prince Edward to Cheshire in the west of England. The Queen gathered an army in the Cheshire region, distributing to the fighting men the young prince's livery—the badge of the Swan. She also summoned friendly lords in other parts of the kingdom to join King Henry at Leicester with as many men as they could raise, as well as supplies and money.

Richard of Warwick marched to his Midlands castle at Warwick, to find his estates plundered and his tenants robbed and harassed by the Lancasterians. Meanwhile, he had word that his father, the Earl of Salisbury, was marching southwest from Yorkshire to meet Queen Margaret's army in Cheshire, and he set out in that direction.

Margaret sent a Lancastrian army of between 6,000 and 7,000, commanded by Lord Audley, to intercept the Earl of Salisbury's force of about 4,000 before either Warwick or the Duke of York could join him. But in spite of their smaller numbers, Salisbury's Yorkists were better trained and disciplined. Marching through southern Cheshire, bound for the town of Ludlow in Shropshire, they reached the village of Market Drayton in the midst of a valley surrounded by hilly country. On the opposite side of the little River Tern, flowing through the valley, the Lancastrians were camped on an elevation.

The Earl of Salisbury did not dare keep on, putting the Lancastrian enemy behind him. He drew his army back about two miles and halted near Blore Heath, beyond a brook the Lancastrians would have to cross to get at him. At dawn the next morning, September 23, 1459, Salisbury led his Yorkists forward through a thick forest that concealed them. When they reached the open heath, a hedge just ahead was high enough to screen them from the enemy, but across the brook they could see the Lancastrian pennants fluttering.

The Earl of Salisbury, though outnumbered, did a masterly job of preparing a defence. He drew up his supply carts into a ring, and behind it his men dug a deep trench for themselves, with sharpened stakes driven into the ground ahead of it.

By that time Queen Margaret's army had discovered the Yorkists. Lord Audley gave the command to attack. His archers advanced first across the brook and sent volley after volley of arrows whistling through the air. They might have done much more damage but for Salisbury's excellent defences. When the Lancastrian archers' ammunition was spent, Lord Audley ordered his cavalry to charge. Meanwhile, although the Queen herself took no part in the battle, she is said to have watched from the tower of a nearby church.

From their well-planned defences, the Yorkist archers now began to fire at the advancing horses. One after another, mounted Lancastrian knights plunged to the earth, their chargers shot from under them.

Lord Audley drew his now disordered Lancastrian troops back, re-formed them and ordered the cavalry to dismount and charge on foot. But most had had enough of the Yorkist archers' sure aim. Not only did they refuse, but many fled, and others—about three hundred, according to one source— to the Earl of Salisbury's Yorkist army. That was the kind of conflict the Wars of the Roses was. More than once, leaders or groups of men changed sides when they thought it would be to their advantage.

The battle lasted for several hours. At last, when their commander, Lord Audley, was killed, the Lancastrian army fled from the field. The Yorkists pursued them for several hours. Sir Thomas and Sir John Neville, the Earl of Warwick's younger brothers, rashly outdistanced their men, found themselves surrounded by Lancastrians and were made prisoners. Just how many were slain is not known, but the Lancastrian losses were severe, and the battlefield gained the name of Deadman's Den among the inhabitants of the region.

Now the Earl of Salisbury could continue his march to Ludlow. There his son, Warwick, and Richard, Duke of York, joined him. But even with these reinforcements, the Yorkists were still weak in numbers. Moreover, the King, marching from Leicester, was now at Worcester, about twenty-five miles southeast of Ludlow, with a large army. Estimates vary, but he probably had at least 10,000 men.

King Henry sent heralds to Ludlow, offering a royal pardon to all Yorkists who would beg forgiveness and swear allegiance to him. When he received no reply, he marched for Ludlow.

The Yorkists had entrenched themselves strongly outside Ludlow. But treachery was at work in their ranks. The Earl of Warwick's six hundred men of the Calais garrison were commanded by Sir Andrew Trollope. He is said to have been corresponding secretly with the young Lancastrian, Henry Beaufort, Duke of Somerset, who offered him a pardon and other rewards if he would desert. At any rate, on the night of October 12, Trollope led the six hundred Calais men over to the Lancastrian camp.

It was a crushing blow to the Yorkists. The Duke of York and the Earls of Salisbury and Warwick decided they could not overcome the King's might in a battle. The Yorkist camp broke up. Richard, Duke of York, with his younger son, the Earl of Rutland, made their way west through the mountain fastnesses of Wales, reached the coast and sailed for Ireland, where York was still Lieutenant.

The Duke of York's elder son, Edward, Earl of March, was entrusted to the Earls of Salisbury and Warwick. They reached Devonshire, on the Channel coast, obtained a ship and sailed for Calais.

With the Yorkist rebellion broken and its leaders scattered, the Lancastrians once more controlled England, but they were far from secure. Although the three Yorkist leaders were refugees, they were still very much alive, able to plot and raise armies.

It would be foolish to say that Henry VI was responsible for the measures taken to prevent the Yorkist leaders from returning. Queen Margaret, that strong, ruthless and determined woman, was still the real ruler of England, and one can only think of poor Henry as a puppet, with Margaret pulling the strings that controlled his every movement.

The Queen summoned a Parliament. To put the escaped Yorkists in peril of their lives if they dared return, she used the bill of attainder. A more vicious device against men's freedom cannot be imagined. Magna Carta, the great document of liberty that King John had signed in 1215, provided that no free man would be imprisoned, exiled or destroyed, or his property taken from him, except by a lawful trial, and that an accused person should be allowed witnesses to testify for him. The bill of attainder violated these provisions. Under it a man could be tried without witnesses, even if he was not there himself, judged guilty, executed or thrown into a prison dungeon for the rest of his life and his property seized. If he had fled the country or was in hiding, he became an outlaw. Anyone could kill him on sight and collect a reward. The very first article of the Constitution of the United States forbids bills of attainder.

Queen Margaret had bills of attainder passed against Richard, Duke of York, his sons the Earls of March and Rutland and the Earls of Salisbury and Warwick. All the ministers the Yorkists had put into office after the first battle of St. Albans were dismissed, and all the laws passed by Parliament after that battle were annulled.

The Queen might take such revenge to her heart's content, but it did her little good. Her Yorkist enemies were already planning a new attempt to destroy the House of Lancaster. In Ireland, where he was very popular with the people, Richard, Duke of York, had been warmly welcomed. Queen Margaret had sent Henry Beaufort, the new Duke of Somerset, to seize Calais, but Richard Neville, Earl of Warwick, his father, the Earl of Salisbury, and young Edward, Earl of March, got there first and drove Somerset off.

During the next months, Warwick corresponded with the Duke of York in Ireland and they began laying their plans. First, Warwick sent Sir John Dynham with a fleet across the Channel, where he raided and sacked the port of Sandwich, seizing most of the ships in the harbour. This lightning foray gave Queen Margaret something to think about.

Warwick, leaving the Earl of Salisbury and another Yorkist supporter, Lord Fauconberg, to hold Calais and guard young Edward of March, went to Ireland. There he conferred with the Duke of York and made final plans for the invasion of England. For the time being the duke was to stay in Ireland. One reason is said to have been that it would not be wise, with his good claim to the throne, to risk his life in battle; another was that Warwick preferred to handle the fighting in England, having a poor opinion of York's military ability.

Queen Margaret, learning that Warwick was in Ireland, sent Henry Holland, the Duke of Exeter, to intercept the earl on his way back to Calais. Unfortunately, the English government had neglected to pay the sailors for some time. They were in an ugly mood and ripe for mutiny. Mutiny they did. When Warwick's vessels hove in sight, the Lancastrian gunners refused to fire their cannon. Warwick contemptuously sailed right by Exeter's fleet to Calais.

Waiting for the time set for the invasion, Warwick sent Dynham over to Sandwich again. The English port did not give up so easily this time, but at last it surrendered. Its commander was captured, taken to Calais and beheaded. Lord Fauconberg and a force were left at Sandwich to hold it as a beachhead for Warwick's invasion. Things were not going well for Queen Margaret and the ~~Yorkists.~~ Lancastrian.

At the end of June, 1460, Warwick, with his father, the Earl of Salisbury, the young Earl of March, other lords and about

1,500 men, landed at Sandwich. They received a great welcome, led by Thomas Bourchier, head of the Church in England as Archbishop of Canterbury. Bourchier was a diplomatic man who always went along with the side that seemed in the most advantageous position.

Volunteers flocked to join Warwick, for this was Kent, where he was beloved and revered almost like a saint. The Yorkist army marched to Canterbury, where the town gates were thrown open to them.

The lords of Kent met Warwick and Salisbury in Canterbury. "We are ready to live and die for you," they promised. "What can we do?"

"I will test your courage," Warwick replied.

With the lords' retainers and all the volunteers, Warwick's army had swelled to a mob of over 6,000 when it marched for London. On July 2 this vast host reached London Bridge. Except that it spanned the Thames, it looked like anything but a bridge. It stretched from Southwark, on the south bank, across to the city, with nineteen arches above the swift flood of the river. Along both sides of it were shops with houses above them, some rising eleven stories high. It was like a miniature city by itself. The houses' upper parts overhung the roadway so that it resembled a dark tunnel.

Preparations had been made to defend the city. Lord Thomas Scales, a Lancastrian official who was hated by the people for his oppressions, had marched into London with an armed force. At the Southwark end of the bridge was a turreted gatehouse, put up for defence. Its iron portcullis gates had been let down to close the entrance, and its turrets manned by soldiers. A drawbridge in the centre, raised when ships passed through, had its gates closed.

A message had been sent ahead to Richard, Earl of Warwick,

warning him not to approach. But the earl returned a reply to the city authorities that persuaded them to take his side, especially since the common people favoured him. Thus, when he and his army reached the gatehouse, they were welcomed by the city aldermen and a crowd of the inhabitants. As they marched across, Warwick's men removed a grisly sight from the turret tops of the gatehouse—the heads of executed Yorkists impaled there on spikes.

A vast crowd was streaming out of London over the bridge. During a rebellion in 1450 it had been partly destroyed by fire, and the repairs had been so poor that there were gaping holes in the roadway. Several men of Warwick's host stepped into them, fell, were unable to rise because of their heavy amour and were trampled to death by the onrushing crowd of welcomers.

Once more King Henry VI had taken positive action instead of the Queen, probably because of Margaret's anxiety for the safety of the little Prince Edward, the Lancastrian heir to the throne. Henry left her with the boy at Coventry and moved east to Northampton, entrusting the defence of London to the hated Lord Thomas Scales and one other lord. But they sought refuge in the Tower of London, leaving Richard, Earl of Warwick, and his associates masters of the city.

Warwick spent a few days in London, feted by the mayor and other officials, but there were the King and his army yet to be reckoned with. Leaving his father, the Earl of Salisbury, and several other lords in charge of London, he marched for Northampton. With him went the Duke of York's young son Edward, Earl of March.

Although the Yorkists did not enjoy it, the heavy rain through which they marched as they approached Northampton, about seventy miles northwest of London, gave them an advantage. The battle of Northampton, a city that in 1460 was, as now, the shire town of Northamptonshire and a centre of the leather trade, was unlike the earlier one at St. Albans, for it was not fought in the town itself. King Henry's army had moved a short distance to a meadow lying between ancient Delapré Abbey and the River Nene, and entrenched itself strongly.

Warwick had brought about 4,000 Yorkists with him. The Lancastrian strength is not known, but it was probably somewhat greater. The King, naturally, did not actively command the Lancastrians. He left that to old Humphrey Stafford, Duke of Buckingham.

Warwick himself commanded the Yorkish army, at the head of its centre, with Lord Fauconberg leading the van, or advance force, and the eighteen-year-old Edward, Earl of March, at the head of the rear guard. As the Yorkists reached a rise overlooking the meadow, Warwick saw the Lancastrians along a line across it, with the river at the north end and the abbey, on a small elevation, at the south. He saw too that, thanks to the rains, the King's large number of cannon in the entrenchments were flooded and useless.

By two o'clock that afternoon, Warwick had formed for an assault. His trumpets sounded a long blast, and he addressed the army.

"Kill all lords, knights and esquires," he ordered, "but spare the King and the common fighting men." Then he signalled to Fauconberg, whose advance force charged down into the meadow, followed by Warwick's force and that of the Duke of York's son, young Edward of March.

Once more treachery was at work, this time in the Lancastrian army. Sir Edmund Grey, commanding its van, suddenly decided his future was better with the Ragged Staff than the royal colours. He led the Lancastrian force over to Warwick's side.

The battle was a fierce, hand-to-hand struggle, though a brief one, lasting only half an hour. For the Lancastrians it was a disaster. They were routed and put to flight. In their frantic rush for safety many of them drowned as they tried to cross the river.

A Yorkist archer suddenly found himself with the greatest prize of all in his grasp—Henry VI. The King, for all his hatred of war, was on the battlefield, even though he took no part in the fighting. He gave himself up to the archer, who took him to the Yorkish leaders. They knelt, did him homage and promised that no harm would come to him.

Warwick's men had obeyed his order before the battle as far as possible. While only about three hundred men were slain on both sides, there were terrible losses among the Lancastrian leaders. Their commander, old Buckingham, lay dead, as well as the Earl of Shrewsbury and many other noble lords who had fought for the King. Young Edward, Earl of March, distinguished himself in this, his first combat.

They took Henry VI into Northampton. Ahead of him rode Richard, Earl of Warwick, carrying the royal sword of state. After staying in Northampton for three days, Warwick, his coleaders and the army escorted Henry to London with every mark of respect. They lodged him in the palace of the Bishop of London.

The two nobles—Lords Scales and Hungerford—whom the King had left to hold London were still in refuge in the Tower. They were already on the verge of starvation. Ships carrying food from Gascony in France, which might have sailed safely up the Thames to the Tower dock, had been captured at sea.

The two lords surrendered to the Yorkists on condition that they be given their freedom.

However, Lord Scales, knowing his unpopularity, did not trust the Yorkists' promise. He obtained a boat and started up the Thames to Westminster, where he could find sanctuary in the abbey and be safe. But a woman recognized him and gave the alarm. Some river boatmen followed, captured and murdered Scales.

The Yorkists were now in control. In no time all the high posts in the government were filled with their followers. A Parliament was summoned to meet at Westminster. And now it was safe for Richard, Duke of York, to leave Ireland and return to England.

Then, foolishly, he seems to have concluded that with Warwick's smashing victory at Northampton he could seize the throne. His claim to it was a very complicated matter, but it was a good one, actually better than that of the Lancastrian, Henry VI. This was all very well, but the Duke of York did not wait to be chosen King in a legal way. In September of that year of 1460 he crossed the Irish Sea, landed near Chester and advanced across England. He reached London on October 10.

He fully expected to be King. He came into London with royal pomp at the head of five hundred men, marching not under the White Rose of York but under the royal arms of England. Trumpets and clarions heralded his coming. He went straight to Westminster, where Parliament was in session.

The Duke of York's trumpets blared as he came into the chamber. At its head stood the throne—vacant, although King Henry VI was still in the capital, while Queen Margaret had fled to safety in Wales with her precious offspring, young Prince Edward.

Richard, Duke of York, strode boldly to the throne and laid

his hand upon its cushion as if he were about to take his seat on it. But there was complete silence in the hall—none of the cheers and acclamations York seems to have expected. He hesitated, suddenly realizing that such a bold action could not give him the support he must have as King. He drew back his hand and stood awkwardly by the throne.

At last Archbishop Bourchier, one of the lords spiritual—members of Parliament representing the clergy, as compared with the lords temporal, who were not in the Church—went up to the duke. With all due reverence he asked, "Would you like to see the King, my lord?"

"I know of no person in this realm the which oweth not to wait on me rather than I on him," the duke replied loftily. Then he turned and left the chamber, but in his exasperation he had to have one petty triumph. The King was then in Westminster Palace, but happened to be occupying the Queen's quarters in her absence. York moved into Henry's own apartments. This sour-grapes kind of action was noised about and won the duke no more popularity.

Nevertheless, York put in a formal claim to the throne before Parliament, tracing his ancestry back to prove his right to it. No one wanted to handle the matter. The lords in Parliament sent it along to King Henry, who dodged making a reply and asked the judges of the high court at Westminster to rule on it. They replied that they had no authority to do so.

At last the lords came up with five objections to Richard of York's claim. The strongest ones were that time after time the duke had taken oaths of allegiance to Henry, acknowledging him as the lawful sovereign of England, and that Parliament had already rejected York's claim and declared the House of Lancaster to be the ruling regime. All this in spite of the Lancastrians' defeat and the new power of the Yorkists.

There was much more argument, and Richard, Duke of York, finally had to accept a compromise. It was agreed that Henry VI was to remain King as long as he lived; then the duke and his heirs would succeed to the throne. Meanwhile, York was to get back his title of Protector.

Henry VI also had to agree to this. There was not much else he could do, for he was practically a prisoner of the Yorkists. They put him back into the Bishop's Palace, and Richard of York took over the one at Westminster, much as if he had been King.

Richard, Earl of Warwick, himself recommended that the duke accept the arrangement. But neither he nor York were through with the Lancastrians. Queen Margaret was at large and using all her power over her supporters to raise an army and gain revenge by driving the Yorkists out. The bloodiest times of the Wars of the Roses were just ahead.

IV

A Warrior Queen's Vengeance

After the disastrous battle of Northampton, Queen Margaret and her little son, Prince Edward, not yet seven years old, went through the most perilous experience of their lives. They escaped westward from Northampton into Cheshire. In the shire's wild southern part, the Queen and her son were suddenly set upon by a band of armed men, who seized her baggage.

Then, as the brigands began to quarrel over the division of the booty, Queen Margaret watched them carefully. Instinct told her that one young man of the band, a more kindly-looking fellow than the others, might be trusted. While the rest bickered over the spoils, she drew him aside.

"I am Queen Margaret," she told him, then pointed to the little prince. "This is the heir to the throne of England. Save the son of your King!"

He believed her, proved loyal and spirited the Queen and little boy away into the craggy mountains of Wales to the west. Near the coast they met two good friends to Lancaster—Henry Holland, Duke of Exeter, and Jasper Tudor, Earl of Pembroke.

The Queen and Henry VI's heir were safe. They sailed for Scotland, where Margaret was welcomed by friendly Queen Mary, widow of James II, the Scottish King.

The north of England was a Lancastrian stronghold, although the Yorkist lords had many estates there. During that autumn of 1460 a group of Lancastrians, led by Henry Percy, Earl of Northumberland, a member of one of the greatest Lancastrian families in England, began pillaging the Yorkist estates. Henry Beaufort, Duke of Somerset, and John Courtenay, Earl of Devon, joined them from the south. They had a powerful army, ready to strike again at the Yorkists.

In London, Richard, Duke of York, heard what was going on. Since the victory at Northampton had been so overwhelming, York did not worry too much about this new Lancastrian threat, and he marched out of London with a small force. He did send young Edward, Earl of March westward to raise more men along the Welsh border, but he left Richard Neville, Earl of Warwick, in London. It was the worst mistake of York's life.

The formidable Lancastrian army made its headquarters at the castle of Pontefract, in what is today the highly industrialized part of Yorkshire surrounding the big manufacturing city of Leeds. There is little to remind one that fountains of blood sprouted within its walls, where many a great lord was beheaded. Only part of its crumbling walls and battlements still stand, and its now dry moat is carpeted with beautiful greensward and planted with shrubs and bright-coloured flowers in summer. Yet there is still something sinister in its appearance to remind the visitor of its dark and bloody history.

On December 20, 1460, the Duke of York and his army reached his castle of Sandal, not far from Pontefract and about a mile from Wakefield, today a bustling manufacturing town.

It appears that Queen Margaret had joined the Lancastrian army at Pontefract and that it was she who suggested an armistice to last over the Christmas holidays until January 8.

York trusted her word and took advantage of the opportunity to send out parties to forage the countryside for food, needed for a possible siege. Thus his small army was further weakened by the absence of these men.

Queen Margaret, if it was she who proposed the holiday truce, broke her word. The Lancastrian army marched out of Pontefract and moved nine miles west to the bridge over the River Calder, on the edge of Wakefield and just north of Sandal Castle. There it drew up in battle array and challenged the Yorkists to come out and fight. Some sources give Margaret credit for commanding the Lancastrians, but the actual leadership is said to have been in the hands of the traitorous Andrew Trollope, who had deserted Richard, Earl of Warwick, at Ludlow.

Edward, Earl of March had not yet reached Yorkshire with the men he had raised on the Welsh borderlands. York's co-leaders advised the duke to stay inside the walls of Sandal and wait in the hope that these badly needed reinforcements would arrive. If it is true that Warwick did not think much of the duke's military talents, he seems to have been right, for the rash Yorkist commander would have no delay. He ordered his army to march out and fight.

The Lancastrians trapped him neatly. The gate of Sandal faced south, while the Lancastrians were drawn up to the north by the bridge. Thus York's army had to wheel around the base of the hill on which the castle stood.

When the Yorkist troops had done so, the duke saw the Lancastrians drawn up ahead of him and ordered his men to charge them. But this Lancastrian force was only their main or centre "battle," as such formations were called. Both Lancastrian wings had been ordered to push forward. As York's men charged, these flank troops closed in behind them. The duke was caught like a fish in a net.

He fought like a madman and so did his troops, but it was completely hopeless. Richard, Duke of York, fell at the head of his men only four hundred yards from the castle. The slaughter among the Yorkists at this battle of Wakefield was frightful. Many lords of the White Rose fell. Trying to escape, York's son, the young Earl of Rutland, was overtaken by the Lancastrian Lord Clifford, a brutal man known as "The Butcher." Their fathers had met in hand-to-hand combat at the first battle of St. Albans, and the elder Clifford had been killed. Now the vengeful younger Clifford said to Rutland, "By God's blood, thy father slew mine, as so will I do thee," and stabbed him to death.

The father of Richard, Earl of Warwick, the Earl of Salisbury, was captured, taken to Pontefract and beheaded. The bodies of the other Yorkist lords slain in the battle were also taken there, their heads chopped off and all—those of the Duke of York, the Earl of Salisbury, the Earl of Rutland and the rest —were set on the battlements. On York's head was placed a paper crown.

This gruesome display had one spot left vacant. That was for Edward, Earl of March, when he arrived. But his head was not destined to join the others there or anywhere else.

Edward, Earl of March, eldest son of the slain Richard, Duke of York, now inherited his father's title, and he, with his cousin Warwick, were the leaders of the Yorkist party. The death of his father at Wakefield was a terrible blow to him, as was the

execution of the Earl of Salisbury to his son Warwick. But the
two young lords were far from beaten, in spite of the devastating Yorkist defeat at Wakefield.

Edward of March, the new Duke of York, was still in the
west, at Gloucester, where he received the dreadful news. He
had been raising men in the countryside, and when he learned
of the Yorkist defeat at Wakefield and of his father's death,
he made even greater efforts and soon had a formidable army.
His intention was to march to London. Victorious Queen
Margaret and her army would surely head for it, and Warwick
was going to need help to hold the capital. But Edward's plans,
for the time being, were suddenly changed.

Margaret had been frantically trying to get aid from Scotland. The canny Scots were willing, for a price, but it was a
high one—Berwick-upon-Tweed.

The River Tweed, flowing eastward into the North Sea,
forms the boundary between England and Scotland in that
part of Britain. Geographically, Berwick should be in Scotland,
for it stands on the north bank of the Tweed, with Scottish
Berwickshire surrounding it. But today Berwick is part of
England. Since it was a thriving seaport in the fifteenth century, it had long been contended for by the two countries,
which were then separately governed. Berwick had changed
hands several times down through the centuries, but in 1461
England held it. Queen Margaret paid the price and gave it to
the Scots, a bargain that did not please the people of England,
especially in the north. In return, Margaret obtained a military
alliance with the Scots.

Powerful help was also on its way to the Queen from another
direction. Her Lancastrian friends, Jasper Tudor, Earl of Pembroke, and James Butler, Earl of Wiltshire, had been raising an

army abroad—in France, Brittany and Ireland—as well as in Wales when they landed there. While Margaret, with her new, strong Lancastrian army, was marching south toward London, the reinforcements the Earls of Pembroke and Wiltshire had assembled were heading west to join them.

Edward of March, the new Duke of York, had also started for London, hoping to cut Margaret off, when he heard of this other Lancastrian army not far from him. He was ahead of them, but with the military brilliance that was to mark his whole career, he instantly turned back.

They met at a little Herefordshire hamlet, Mortimer's Cross. According to one of the old chroniclers, as Edward's army approached the place on the morning of February 2, 1461, his superstitious men were terrified to see in the eastern sky not one, but three suns. It was some sort of mirage or reflection due to the weather conditions, but to Edward's men it was an omen of doom.

Save for the new Duke of York's ingenuity and quick thinking, his army might have fled before reaching Mortimer's Cross. But Edward of March halted his Yorkists and addressed them.

"Be of good comfort and dread not," he said. "This is a good sign, for these three suns betoken the Father, the Son and the Holy Ghost. And therefore, let us have a good heart, and in the name of Almighty God go against our enemies."

In a trice he had turned dread to confidence in the hearts of his men and made them see the phenomenon in the sky as an omen of victory. Edward knelt and gave thanks to God, and then he and his army marched on to Mortimer's Cross.

There, in a swampy area called Wig Marsh, Edward concealed his army, knowing the Lancastrians were heading that way from Hereford. The size of each army is not known, but from an estimate of the casualties in the battle, both must have been quite large, with Edward's force probably somewhat the larger.

As the Lancastrians approached the marsh, the Yorkists burst from their concealment and swooped down on them. Young Edward, Duke of York, tall, strong and handsome, must have been an inspiring figure as he led them into battle. The crest on his polished helmet was a coronet with a tuft of azure feathers, and the livery he and his men wore was a white lion. His battle standard was a blazing sun. Certainly he did inspire his men, for they fell upon the Lancastrians like an army of tigers, killing many and routing the rest. One chronicle says that 3,000 men lay dead on the field after the short battle, and probably most were Lancastrians.

The Earl of Pembroke, Jasper Tudor, and the Earl of Wiltshire managed to escape in disguise, but Jasper's old father, Owen, who had been with him, was captured. The Yorkists took him into the town of Hereford. In its centre was one of the crosses so common in market towns of those days, and still to be seen in many old towns today.

There they beheaded Owen Tudor. The old man did not believe they would execute him, for after the death of Henry V he had married that King's widow, Catherine of Valois, daughter of King Charles VI of France. Only when he saw them bring up a block and axe and tear the red velvet collar of his doublet off did he wail, "That head shall lie on the stock that was wont to lie on Queen Catherine's lap!"

When his head had been chopped off, it was placed on the topmost step of the pedestal on which the market cross stood. Then, according to one chronicler, a "mad woman" sponged the blood from the head, combed the hair and placed over a hundred lighted candles around the market cross. Seven Lancastrian knights who had been captured were also beheaded there. This was the victors' way in this barbarous series of wars.

Once more the Yorkists had scored a great victory, but it was not enough to stop iron-willed Queen Margaret. She and her Lancastrian army, under the turncoat Andrew Trollope, were marching through eastern England for London, and here the worst pillaging of the wars took place. They cut a swath of devastation thirty miles wide as they advanced.

Villages were burned, towns, churches and abbeys looted of everything of value they contained, interiors of stone manor houses put to the torch, men tortured to reveal where their money was, women mistreated. And while no one could stand against the Queen's army, all this stirred a hatred for her, Henry VI and Lancaster that would never die. Yet probably Margaret of Anjou could not prevent it. This was more of the payment she had to make to have her revenge upon the Yorkists and destroy them. The Scots, Welshmen, a few French and some from the north of England who made up her host were in it for what it would bring them. They cared little whether Lancaster or York ruled England.

The Queen was well on her way when Richard, Earl of Warwick, heard of her march and knew she must be heading for London. The earl had no army to speak of, since the dead Richard, Duke of York, had taken the main Yorkist force north with him. But London, being on the whole favourable to the Yorkists at this time, aided Warwick in hastily assembling an army, and of course he could depend upon fiercely loyal Kent, just to the southeast, to furnish others. He is estimated to have had about 30,000 men by the time he marched out of

London. Queen Margaret's Lancastrian army was probably larger, since she is believed to have had about 40,000 men when she began her southward journey.

Warwick decided not to let the King out of his hands and leave him in London, so he took Henry along. The Yorkist army reached St. Albans on February 12, 1461, well ahead of the advancing Lancastrians. This gave Warwick time to prepare one of the strongest and most unusual defences ever known up to that time in England.

He spread his Yorkists in three divisions over a long line, extending from the northern outskirts of St. Albans across low-lying ground up to an area known as "No Man's Land." Some of his men were armed with "hand guns" from Burgundy, never before seen in England. They shot either pellets of lead—actually bullets—or arrows an ell (nearly four feet) long, tipped with iron and "wildfire," a highly inflammable mixture of chemicals which would burst into flame when the arrow struck. Warwick also had cannon.

As for the Yorkist archers, they carried enormous nail-studded shields called pavises, with swinging doors that the bowmen could open to fire their arrows and then close again. Once their ammunition was gone they could cast the pavises before them so the nails might prevent an enemy from hurling himself upon them. The army also had great nets studded with nails, used to protect the weak parts of the line. To keep enemy horsemen from charging through open spaces in hedges, lattices studded with nails were set up in the openings. Still another defensive weapon was the caltrop, or hedgehog, a star-shaped piece of iron with four sharp points that could be sown over the ground to menace approaching men and horses.

Warwick had four days to prepare before Margaret's army

approached. But something happened that was so common it might have been expected. In spite of Kent's strong loyalty, the leader of one Kentish detachment turned traitor. He sent the Queen full details of how Warwick's army was drawn up, and also seems to have offered to desert with his men and join the Lancastrians at the right moment.

The Lancastrians were on a direct collision course with Warwick's Yorkists. When Queen Margaret learned of the earl's strong position, she swung her army west to Dunstable, a dozen miles northwest of St. Albans, then turned toward it down Watling Street. This was done with all possible speed to prevent Warwick's scouts from reporting the change. If it succeeded, the Queen might take the Yorkists by surprise around their left flank.

Succeed it did. The Lancastrians took a Yorkist post at Dunstable by surprise and killed or captured every man. Then the Queen's army made a night march and approached St. Albans about three o'clock in the morning. So complete was the surprise that when the Lancastrians marched into the old town the street barriers had not been set up. It was not until they reached the marketplace at the entrance to St. Peter's Street that the garrison Warwick had stationed in the town was alarmed.

However, the garrison's bowmen launched such a deadly attack that the Lancastrian advance guard was driven back to the River Ver, at the southwest end of the town. But Margaret's scouts discovered a roundabout, unguarded route to the north, and by it the Lancastrian army swarmed into St. Peter's Street.

Nevertheless, the Yorkists held one advantage. Warwick's army was fresh, while Queen Margaret's, having marched most of the night, was tired. The left wing of Warwick's army moved into St. Peter's Street and met the Lancastrians in fierce struggle. Once more the Yorkist archers, with their queer but effective great shields, took terrible toll of their enemies. The Yorkists' new hand guns too were used with deadly effect. Things did not look well for Margaret of Anjou.

But more and more of her big Lancastrian army was pouring in, while so far only Warwick's left wing had been in the fight. Nothing had been heard or seen of the Yorkist centre and right wing, and now the left one was in trouble. Its line broke and it fled in panic before the superior numbers of the Lancastrians.

Warwick had ridden back to bring his centre division into the battle. But his pleas went unheeded. Seeing the left wing in flight, the Yorkists in the centre joined them, except for the traitorous Kentishman and his force, who promptly went over to the Lancastrian side.

Warwick fought valiantly and did what he could to bring up his last hope, the right wing, reorganize it and continue the battle. He did manage to establish a defence line of sorts and stand off the Lancastrians until dusk. But there was no hope that he could still win the next morning. He had only about 4,000 of his 30,000 left; the rest were scattered far and wide in flight.

Knowing this remnant would be annihilated the next day, Warwick managed to skirt around the enemy and retreat west to Chipping Norton, in the Cotswold Hills of Oxfordshire. There he met Edward, Duke of York, fresh from his victory at Mortimer's Cross.

Before this second battle of St. Albans, Warwick had moved King Henry as far away as possible, lest he fall into the hands of his wife and her army. The victorious Lancastrians found the simple-minded monarch sitting under an oak tree, singing songs. Henry VI, Queen Margaret and their young son, Prince Edward, met in joyous reunion for the first time in many months. The jubilant Henry knighted his seven-year-old son on the spot, and all went to the abbey of St. Albans for the night. The King issued an order that the town was to be spared, but the looting rabble the Queen had brought with her from the north paid no attention, and St. Albans too was sacked.

The King and Queen gave their son an early lesson in ruthlessness. As usual, there were some captured Yorkist lords, and three were beheaded. Little Prince Edward was made to preside over the court-martial that quickly condemned them.

The Lancastrians then started for London. But although Margaret had taken her revenge in no uncertain manner at Wakefield and the second battle of St. Albans, they were refused admittance to the walled capital. The London authorities were ready to welcome them, but the citizens, having heard of the devastation the Queen's army had wreaked to the north, were not.

So Queen Margaret went north once more, her army again pillaging on the way. Her only real triumph was to have recovered the King. The Wars of the Roses and her struggle for supremacy were not over yet—far from it.

V

A Yorkist King Rules England

They called Edward of March "The White Rose of Rouen" after the capital of Normandy, where he had been born. At that time his father, Richard, Duke of York, was there as Lieutenant of France—an empty title, since England was fast losing its possessions in that country.

Now, in 1461, though Edward, the new Duke of York, was only in his twentieth year, the traits that were to mark his future were already to be seen in him—his great strength, stature of more than six feet, good looks, engaging manners, complete self-confidence and genius as a leader of men in battle. He had his faults as well—a lack of the knowledge of politics and government a good ruler required, too much love of pleasure and too much trustfulness at a time when many of the great lords of England were not to be trusted. Most fortunately for him, he had Richard Neville, Earl of Warwick, with him, a master politician who loved the scheming, maneuvering and diplomacy that were so much needed.

The two met there at Chipping Norton in the lovely Cotswold Hills, sheep-raising country and no doubt as enchanting a place as it is today, when it attracts many tourists. Edward and Warwick called a council of their coleaders, and the earl told them of the disaster at the second battle of St. Albans.

"Where is the King?" Duke Edward asked.

"_You_ are the King," Warwick replied.

"Why so, good Richard?"

"Because he who has been King and so weak a one is no longer fit to rule. Margaret of Anjou has taken him and their Lancastrian army north, for London will have none of them. I swear to you, my lord Edward, that if you march for it at once you will be acclaimed King. The people are tired of a sovereign who cannot govern. And your right to the throne by descent cannot be challenged."

"But the Lancastrians are not subdued," Edward objected. "I have no money for waging war. The lords who support me have paid their expenses out of their own purses."

"Have no fears, my lord Edward," replied Warwick. "Let us march to London. You will have the people's support there —and that of the merchants, who will be ready to lend you money. Accept the throne, and then we will crush the Lancastrians."

London had been terrified at the news from St. Albans. Everyone had expected the Queen's victorious army to besiege and probably overrun the capital. Shops were shut up, and many people kept to their houses, hiding their valuables; some patrolled the city walls with what arms they had. Cecily Neville, widow of the slain Richard, Duke of York, and mother of the new duke, Edward of March, fled by ship to the Low Countries with Edward's younger brothers, George and Richard.

The relief caused by the withdrawal of the Lancastrian army northward was as nothing to news on February 23, 1461, which electrified the city. No one had known where the defeated Richard Neville, Earl of Warwick, was. Captured, said some, which almost surely meant his execution. Escaped across the Channel to Calais, said others. Still others believed he was in hiding somewhere near London.

Now word came that Warwick, very much alive, had joined forces with Edward, Duke of York, and was marching toward London! On the 27th the two Yorkist leaders entered the city, its gates thrown open in welcome.

The streets were jammed with joyous, shouting people. It must have been an inspiring sight—Edward the new Duke of York in his shining armour and blue-feather-crested helmet, prancing along with Warwick on their great chargers, the Blazing Sun standard borne before them. Behind them, lords, knights, esquires, archers and men-at-arms, Duke Edward's proudly displaying the badge of the White Lion, the red-jacketed earl's men the Ragged Staff, while his banner flaunted not only the Ragged Staff but the Bear which was part of his standard. London went mad.

The two Yorkists went first to the palace of the Bishop of London, close to St. Paul's, then to Baynard's Castle, near the bank of the Thames where the little Fleet River flowed into it. There the great question was discussed—how was Edward to be made King?

A plan was agreed upon: Warwick's brother, George Neville, Bishop of Exeter, had been made chancellor by the Yorkists after their victory at Northampton. This lofty official called a meeting of the citizens at St. John's Fields, Clerkenwell, just outside the city walls to the northwest.

There Chancellor Neville, who had a smooth tongue, told the people of all that Henry VI had done (or in most cases not done) that made him unfit to rule England. Then he explained Duke Edward's just claim to the throne by right of descent from King Edward III.

Then the chancellor asked the multitude: "Do you declare Edward, Duke of York and Earl of March, your true and worthy King?"

A tremendous roar went up: "Yea! Yea!"

With this approval, a delegation that included Warwick, other Yorkist lords and leading knights, high-ranking clergy and prominent citizens of London called upon Duke Edward at Baynard's Castle.

"Your party of the House of York and the commons have chosen you as their King," they told him.

With becoming modesty, Edward objected: "I am too young to be King. I feel myself scarcely able to bear such a great and responsible burden."

Three high prelates of the Church—the Archbishop of Canterbury and the bishops of Salisbury and Exeter—then pressed Edward to accept. Having duly shown his humility, Edward then agreed to what he had come to London to obtain. First he knelt and thanked God for the honour that had been thrust upon him; then expressed his gratitude to his followers and the people who had approved his bowing to the will of the Almighty.

On March 4, 1461, Edward rode in pomp and glory to St. Paul's. There the chancellor preached, and then all moved on to Westminster Hall, a part of the great Palace of Westminster, seat of the English government. This ancient structure, completed in 1099 by King William Rufus and remodelled in 1402, stood on the bank of the Thames, outside and upriver from the City. In this hallowed place stood the throne.

Edward marched through the vast hall and took his seat on the throne. In addition to his noble followers and their retinues, a multitude of the common people jammed every nook and cranny of the place. Then Edward himself explained his right to claim the style and authority of a king.

Again the people were asked if they accepted him, and again they roared, "Yea! Yea!" The sound billowed and echoed among the huge beams of the hall's arched roof.

Next Edward and all of the rest went to adjoining Westminster Abbey. There, in a ceremony conducted by the high prelates of the Church, the sceptre of Edward the Confessor, who had built the Abbey, was presented to the new King. Now no longer Edward, Earl of March and Duke of York, but King Edward IV, he did homage at the altar and shrine of the Confessor and sat down on the throne that stood there. And thus did Richard Neville, Earl of Warwick, gain the name by which he became widely known—"The Kingmaker."

Edward IV was both king and not a king. One part of the ceremony had not yet been carried out. The golden crown had not been placed on his head. Edward was in truth the new ruler of southern England, very largely loyal to the House of York, but the northern part of the kingdom, leaning strongly toward the Lancastrians, had not been subdued. The new King made a solemn vow that his coronation would not be held until Henry VI and Margaret of Anjou had been either put to death or banished forever, and the House of Lancaster utterly crushed.

London rejoiced. Someone devised a saying that became popular and was constantly repeated: "Let us walk in a new vineyard, and let us make a gay garden with this fair white rose and herb, the Earl of March."

He lost no time in moving to accomplish the downfall of the Lancastrians. He sent messengers throughout eastern England with a proclamation: "It is the King's purpose to reform the hurts and mischief and griefs that reign in this land." And he summoned all loyal followers to come to London, ready to march under the royal standard. He also dispatched Warwick to the Midlands to raise men.

Supporters from Kent, Surrey, East Anglia and other eastern counties flocked in. Just a week after Edward had been proclaimed King, Lord Fauconberg marched out of London with the advance division of the army. Two days later, on March 13, the King himself set out with the rest. As his Yorkist army passed through ravaged St. Albans, the streets were lined with people. A shout went up: "Dear Sire, venge us on King Henry and his wife!"

Reinforcements poured in all along the northward route. Lord Thomas Stanley, who with his brother, Sir William Stanley, had great power in the western shires of Lancashire and Cheshire, joined Edward with four hundred archers. Warwick came in with his detachment under the Ragged Staff badge. It was a big army. Just how large, historians disagree. One says there were 48,000, but this appears far too large. Another respected writer estimates it at between 15,000 and 20,000, with a more cautious one putting it as little as 10,000. Probably 20,000 is a fair estimate. It was still considerably smaller than Margaret of Anjou's great Lancastrian horde in the north, the largest army in any battle of the Wars of the Roses, though undisciplined and badly trained.

When Margaret heard of Edward's approach, she drew up

her army near the village of Towton in Yorkshire, about fifteen miles north of Wakefield. The Yorkist army reached Ponte-fract, a dozen miles southeast of Towton, on the 27th or 28th of March.

There was a furious clash on the 28th between advance parties of both armies. A Yorkist detachment had been stationed at Ferrybridge, not far from Pontefract, on the banks of the River Aire. When the Lancastrians learned of it, Lord Clifford, "The Butcher," who had slain the young Earl of Rutland after the battle of Wakefield, led a force against the Yorkists. This minor battle was a bitter struggle, lasting six hours. At last King Edward brought up his main body. Then the Lancastrian detachment was almost destroyed and the Yorkists got revenge upon Clifford. He removed his helmet for a moment during the fight, and in that instant a Yorkist arrow transfixed him through the throat and he fell dying to the ground.

On Palm Sunday morning, March 29, the skies had the leaden look that foretokens snow, and a bitter wind was blowing. Nevertheless, Edward IV's army marched over the Yorkshire plain to the Lancastrians' position. The battle of Towton was really fought between that village and Saxton, to the south of it, on bleak moorland or heath, with several low ridges running through it. Queen Margaret's Lancastrian army was drawn up on one ridge, with the Cock Beck (a beck being a little stream, usually with a rocky bottom) to the west of it.

Since it was Palm Sunday, pious Henry VI did not want to fight. "Let there be a truce until tomorrow," he said, "for this holy and solemn day should be kept religiously, not in bloody combat."

Margaret of Anjou and her commanders knew the Yorkists

were not going to wait until Monday, so no one paid any attention to him. Henry stayed in his tent during the battle, saying the beads of his rosary.

Not that his participation could have changed the course of the conflict, anyhow. The chief of Margaret's able commanders was twenty-four-year-old Henry Beaufort, Duke of Somerset and son of the one killed in the first battle of St. Albans. There were also Henry Percy, Earl of Northumberland, Lord Ralph Dacre of Gillesland, the treacherous Sir Andrew Trollope, commanding the advance force, and other lords.

For a time the two armies simply stayed where they were, the Yorkists on a small ridge opposite that of the enemy. By about eleven, snow began to whip over the desolate Yorkshire moors, borne on the wings of an icy wind and driving straight into the faces of the Lancastrians. Lord Fauconberg, at the head of the Yorkist front line, seized this advantage, knowing it would be difficult for the Lancastrian archers to see their foes.

"Fire a single arrow each and then fall back out of range," he ordered his bowmen.

His strategem produced exactly the effect he had hoped for. The Lancastrian bowmen retaliated, each firing several arrows. Since the snow made it impossible for them to see that their targets had drawn back, the shafts struck harmlessly into the ground.

Then Fauconberg ordered his archers: "Advance and pick up the arrows." And expecting that the enemy's bombardment would be followed by an assault from the Lancastrian billmen and men-at-arms, he added, "Leave enough of them sticking in the ground to impede the enemy's advance."

His belief was right, for the enemy began a charge up the

slope of the ridge. Not only did Fauconberg's archers have an extra supply of enemy arrows, but those left in the ground at a slant did inconvenience the foe's advance. The real battle was on—no matter of clever military maneuvering and strategy, but a fierce hand-to-hand combat to the death—with the crown of England at stake.

The slaughter in this bloodiest and biggest of all battles in the Wars of the Roses was indescribable. Above the howl of the wind rose the crash of battleaxes, the deadly, crushing thud of leaden mallets and the clash of swords and daggers. Men fell dead instantly; others, dying or wounded, shrieked and moaned. One chronicle has it that a wall of the dead and dying men of both sides was gradually built up, impeding the living from getting at each other.

Most of the fighting, even by the nobles who had horses, was done on foot. Warwick rode up to Edward, dismounted, killed his horse with his sword and cried, "Let him flee that will, for surely I will tarry with him that will tarry with me." And in token of this as a solemn oath, he kissed his sword.

The battle raged for hours, with the superior numbers of the Lancastrians finally beginning to tell against the Yorkists. But Edward's army did not yet have its full strength in the fight. The force raised in East Anglia by John Mowbray, Duke of Norfolk, had not come up from the rear of the long column which had marched to the battlefield. At last it appeared, joining the Yorkist right flank.

It turned the tide. King Edward and Warwick, with their men, drove a wedge into the centre of the Lancastrian line, and its left portion was gradually pushed back by Norfolk's men across the Saxton-Towton road and up the slope behind it, where it was cut to pieces.

On the opposite side, the Lancastrian right wing of Henry Percy, Earl of Northumberland, was doing better. It pushed the Yorkist left wing back until many of the troops broke and fled. But, as has happened in more than one battle, the Lancastrians made the mistake of giving chase, taking them out of the fight. Margaret of Anjou's army had lost both its right and left wings.

Edward IV then hurled his men against the remaining centre of the Lancastrian line. It was late in the afternoon, but before nightfall the Yorkists had put the enemy to flight over its only possible escape route—the road running northwest from Towton to Tadcaster.

There was only one obstacle, a ford across the little Cock Beck, ordinarily only a brook, but now swollen to a torrent by the constant rains of that season. The ford was a narrow one, and the press of Lancastrians running for their lives so great that many were pushed into the deeper water and drowned in the flood.

The battle was over. Again, the accounts vary as to how many were killed. Some estimates run higher than 30,000. It does appear likely, however, that the Lancastrians lost about half of their army, and for the time being they were utterly crushed. Henry VI and Margaret of Anjou fled north into Scotland for refuge. Dead on the field lay many a lord. The Lancastrians suffered most severely in this respect too. Henry Percy, Earl of Northumberland, Lord Dacre and the infamous Andrew Trollope were among those slain. The young Duke of Somerset escaped with his life to remain a peril to the House of York.

Edward ordered the execution of all Lancastrian lords who had been captured. Thomas Courtenay, Earl of Devon, was executed when the King went to York the next day, and his head was set on the city gates at the spot where that of Edward's father, the Duke of York, had been put after the battle of Wakefield. Later, John Butler, Earl of Wiltshire, was caught trying to reach Scotland. His head was sent to be impaled on London Bridge.

Now that the Lancastrians had been shattered and the House of York had a control of sorts over the north, Edward could think of being crowned. But first, after staying a fortnight in York, he went north to Durham in the shire of that name, then on to Newcastle in Northumberland. From there he turned south and then west on a leisurely journey that took him through Lancashire and Cheshire; from there he went east through the Midlands, visiting many towns on the way. This was known as a "progress," often used by English rulers during their reigns, not only to gain goodwill by showing themselves to the people, but to impress them with the power of the Crown.

When the King reached Stony Stratford in Buckinghamshire, he paused for a couple of days at the nearby mansion of Grafton, the residence of Richard Woodville, Lord Rivers. It was a little strange, considering that the Woodvilles were Lancastrians, and Lord Rivers' eldest daughter, Dame Elizabeth, was a widow whose husband, Sir John Grey, had been killed at the second battle of St. Albans, fighting with Queen Margaret's Lancastrian army.

However, it would seem that Lord Rivers was ready to go along with the now powerful Yorkists, and King Edward gave him a royal pardon as a result of the visit. No one appears to have realized what was probably the real reason behind this forgiveness. Warwick, who had remained in the north, knew nothing of it, of course, but there is no reason to think he would have seen anything ominous about it.

Then Edward IV and his followers rode on. London would long remember his entrance into the city on June 16. The King's two younger brothers, George, who was eleven, and Richard, eight, had been summoned back to England from their exile in the Low Countries, where they had been taken by their mother after Queen Margaret's triumph in the second battle of St. Albans. They rode beside their great and famous brother in the procession.

One can imagine the two boys' excitement as the cavalcade passed through broad Cheapside, lined with the shops of grocers, mercers, haberdashers, ironmongers, hosiers, shoe-makers, pepperers, poulterers and the gorgeous establishments of the goldsmiths, their fronts gilded and painted in many colours, each with its sign suspended from a long pole jutting into the street. And all along Cheapside, thousands of people lined the way, cheering themselves hoarse for King Edward. There was colour in the procession itself—not only the magnificence of the army with its banners and liveries, but the scarlet robes of the mayor and aldermen of London and the green apparel of four hundred prominent citizens.

That night there was more excitement and glory for the two boys. Their royal brother created them, and twenty-six others, Knights of the Bath, with all the ritual and ceremony that went with the award of this high honour. And the next day, clad in the blue robes, white hoods and strips of white silk over their shoulders that were the costume of this order, they rode with their brother to his coronation in Westminster Abbey.

It must have been awesome to them, this solemn ceremony

in the great church where all the rulers of England had been crowned since 1066. First, before all the high-ranking and common people who had pushed into the abbey until its doors would admit no more, the Archbishop of Canterbury cried, "Do you consent to the coronation of King Edward IV?" The roar of acclamation that went up seemed to shake the mighty stone foundations of the church.

Then Edward took his oath of office and lay prostrate before the altar as his sumptuous purple robes were laid aside and he was anointed with holy oil. Finally, seated on the throne, Edward had St. Edward the Confessor's golden crown placed upon his head.

At last, Edward IV could truly call himself King of England. Yet if the throne had teetered a little as he sat down, it would not have been strange. Henry VI and Margaret of Anjou were in exile, and while Henry might have been resigned to the loss of his crown, his tough and indomitable queen was not yet beaten, small though her chances of regaining power seemed. And although King Edward had subdued the north, its turbulent people were not ones to remain so for long.

After the coronation there was a lavish banquet in Westminster Hall, with food and drink of all kinds in great abundance, including such delicacies as swans, peacocks and pheasants. All was merry, and on the following day the King used his royal powers to confer dukedoms on both his brothers. George was named Duke of Clarence, and Richard Duke of Gloucester.

Yet trouble was still brewing from the beaten but not hopeless Lancastrians. Shakespeare spoke truly when he wrote in *King Henry IV:* "Uneasy lies the head that wears a crown."

VI

An Indomitable Queen Fights On

King Edward's reign began in comparative peace. He had been through so much fighting and so many long, weary marches before he gained the throne that he wanted to enjoy himself for a time. There were forests all around London, and he spent much time there pursuing his favourite sport of hunting, as well as falconry, in which keen-eyed, fierce falcons with their powerful hooked beaks swoop out of the sky to pounce upon game birds, hares and other small animals. The new King was also constantly entertained by nobles, wealthy merchants and other citizens, all anxious to show their loyalty and goodwill.

What kind of an England was it over which King Edward IV had come to reign? London, of course, was the centre of the realm, with somewhere between 50,000 and 75,000 people, four times as many as its nearest rivals, York and Bristol. All the main roads in the kingdom led to one or another of the five gates in the walls around the city, erected by England's ancient Roman conquerors.

It was the great centre of trade too. Its harbour in the Thames

River was crowded with ships of many nations. The Thames was the city's chief highway as well, for there was so much traffic in the streets, most of which were narrow, that it was easier to travel by water—especially to Westminster, a short distance upriver, with its palace, the buildings where Parliament and the high courts sat and ancient, hallowed Westminster Abbey. To reach Westminster, one passed under London Bridge, among the wonders of the world.

The city had its fine buildings and residences, many churches, including great St. Paul's Cathedral, and three royal palaces—the fortress-prison-palace of the Tower of London, Baynard's Castle and the Wardrobe. There were two or three main streets, the chief one being Cheapside, but most of them were narrow and crooked and made dark by the overhanging gables of the houses. There lived the masses in want and misery in dark, rat- and vermin-infested hovels, and in the stench of garbage and refuse thrown into the only sewer the metropolis had—the street, where kites and ravens were the only garbage collectors.

England had a number of other prosperous cities, mostly very ancient, but nine-tenths of the population was rural. These peasant farmers were different from the serfs of the preceding centuries, who had been half enslaved to the lords of the great manors whose land they occupied. The age of feudalism was almost dead.

Many of the new class of farmers were called yeomen and owned their own land, others were still tenants of the lords, paying rent for their land—but almost all were freemen. The landlord was still powerful, but his tenants had new freedoms which enabled them to overcome the tyranny under which so many had formerly lived. In the manor courts where the landlord or his steward, who managed his affairs, settled disputes and minor violations of the law, the tenants had a deciding voice.

Farming itself had changed greatly. In the earlier centuries crops and dairy products produced most of the revenue; now it was sheep. Wool and cloth were England's largest and most profitable product, although iron, tin and lead mining also flourished.

At first, wool was primarily exported to other countries to be made into cloth. Then weaving increased, and since English cloth was of the finest quality, the merchants could make a greater profit by exporting it than by selling raw wool. Craftsmen in the rural districts who owned their own hand looms wove the wool into cloth, which was then collected and passed on to other craftsmen for finishing.

There were still the very poor who occupied the ancient hovels of wattle-and-daub—interwoven twigs mixed with mud or clay—but most of the common people lived in better houses than formerly. And though the children of a poor peasant still had little chance for schooling, those of the yeomen in the rural areas and the burghers in the towns who were freemen could often attend a free school. Or their sons might be apprenticed and learn a trade which could lead to prosperity.

As for the nobility and rich, untitled gentry of England, the new prosperity had improved their living conditions greatly. Nobles lived either in greatly enlarged and improved manor houses or in the many castles all over England.

Most sons of lords and rich gentry were sent away from home to be educated. The scholarly Henry VI had founded famous Eton, a forerunner of the English public schools. Latin was the chief subject, but other accomplishments were considered of great importance to a young gentleman—riding, jousting in tournaments, hunting, dancing, playing the harp and pipes and singing.

England's two important universities, Oxford and Cambridge, were growing in size and influence. Libraries were established there, as well as two in London.

Because of its prosperity, fifteenth-century England was a time of extravagant dress. Velvet, satin, silk, damask, fine linen and costly furs were worn by all who could afford them. And milord's plumage was as colourful and extreme as milady's.

The most important new style for men was the doublet. It was a short jacket, coming to the waist, replacing the long gowns, now worn only at solemn ceremonies. Sleeves, which had been enormously wide and so long that their ends often touched the ground, now came only to the waist, and were slashed so that the men's white shirts showed through. Often doublets were cut open in front to show the stomacher, a corset-like piece of bright-coloured cloth, worn also by women and often richly embroidered and studded with jewels. The men wore long hose which came all the way to the waist.

Men's shoes, in the early part of the fifteenth century, were so ridiculous that their wearers must have looked like strange creatures out of some fairy tale, or perhaps men from Mars. The toes had points which were sometimes as much as two feet long. Later this fashion gave way to shoes so enormously broad that they too were preposterous. Men wore gloves; ladies did not.

Women still wore the long gowns that had been in style earlier. They were very heavy because so much material was used, and they had long trains trimmed with furs. Much fur was worn, especially sable, ermine and miniver, the white fur of the Siberian squirrel, luxurious then but little heard of today.

Women's hair is called their crowning glory, and in the fifteenth century it was something to marvel at. Women of fashion wore fantastic headdresses. In one style, called the "tower" or "steeple," the hair was built up on many rolls of linen into a tower that was sometimes two feet high. Another, called the "mitre," was shaped much like the tall, pointed hats worn then and today by prelates of the Church. Still another headdress projected from each side of the head in a kind of frame, ending in a point, which gave it the name of the "horned headdress."

Extreme styles and luxury of dress in prosperous England became so widespread that royalty and nobility grew jealous of such airs when they were put on by those of lower standing. When Edward IV came to the throne, he re-established the so-called sumptuary laws, which had lapsed after being in effect in the fourteenth century. They defined what sort of clothes, cloth, fur, colour and style different ranks of people could wear.

In 1461, that first year of Edward IV's reign, the king made another "progress" as autumn and harvest time approached, a season of rejoicing and good feeling among the country people. This time it was to show himself to his subjects in the friendly south of England, as well as the west and the Midlands.

He went southeastward first through Kent, visiting towns and villages all along the way, including the holy shrine of Canterbury, then along the Channel coast to Hastings and nearby Battle Abbey, where William the Conqueror, invading from Normandy, had defeated King Harold II and subdued all the kingdom, completely changing the course of England's history.

Proceeding westward through Sussex and Hampshire to Salisbury in Wiltshire, the King turned northwest to Bristol, then on through Gloucestershire and finally back to London through the Midlands. He had cause to feel that all was well in those parts of the realm, for the people all welcomed him joyously, pledged allegiance and entertained and presented him with costly gifts.

All *was* well in the south, but the north was restless, with many Lancastrian supporters itching for a chance to renew the struggle with the Yorkists. However, the King was confident on that score. His friend Richard Neville, Earl of Warwick, a mighty pillar of support, was there, ready to stamp out the slightest sign of new rebellion.

It seemed a little odd that Warwick, the Kingmaker, had not even come south for Edward's coronation. Some believed that he did not want the King to outshine him in London. Not that the earl had aspirations for the throne himself, for he seems not to have coveted it. In fact, although the new monarch showered honours upon his supporters and it would have been natural for Warwick to have been given a dukedom, he was not. No doubt he could have had it, but he seems to have been satisfied to remain the Earl of Warwick. It was the title under which he had become famous; he was known by it everywhere, and it was a symbol of power and renown to the English people.

Nevertheless, Warwick loved fame. And in London, not only would Edward be the centre of attention for all as he was crowned, but his military successes surpassed Warwick's. At the second battle of St. Albans the earl had been soundly beaten, while Edward had routed the Lancastrians at Mortimer's Cross. Then, at Towton, Edward had commanded, and smashed the Lancastrians to pieces, while Warwick's conduct in the battle, according to some historians, had been far from glorious. The Kingmaker was never the great military man that Edward was. His great talent lay in government and in the intrigues and maneuvering of diplomacy. Yet in all fairness to him, he was needed in the north to control its unruly people.

Warwick made his headquarters at the favourite of his many estates, Middleham Castle, although for more than three years he was all over the north, putting down uprisings that often took place and keeping the Scottish allies of the Lancastrians in check when they crossed the border on raids.

King Edward decided that his younger brothers, Richard, now Duke of Gloucester, and George, the new Duke of Clarence, should have instruction in the knightly accomplishments they would need when they grew up. The King sent them to Middleham to be tutored under the charge of his dear friend Warwick.

Middleham Castle was in northwestern Yorkshire on wild and lonely moorlands. In that year of 1461 it had stood for three hundred years, where its ruins stand today, at the top of a steep slope rising from the village of Wensleydale in the valley of the swift-flowing River Ure. Built of gray stone, its central building, or keep, was one of the largest of all English castles. Surrounding it, within encircling walls from ten to twelve feet thick, and its moat, were other buildings, including fortifications with towers, a mill and a bakehouse. On the castle's eastern side, across a drawbridge over the moat, was a large courtyard lined with stables, a smithy and a slaughterhouse.

There, for the next three years under guardianship of Warwick, the Kingmaker, Richard, Duke of Gloucester, spent what were probably the happiest days of his life. It is well to know something of his youth, because of all the royalty and nobility who took part in the Wars of the Roses he is the most famous, and his name possibly the most unfairly blackened and disgraced.

For a good many years some things that were almost certainly not true were believed of him, as well as others which may or may not have been true. It was said that he was a puny hunchback with a withered arm, and that he was called Richard Crouchback. There is no reliable evidence to show that he either was a hunchback or had a withered arm—or that, while he lived, he was known as Crouchback. The nearest he came to deformity seems to be that his right arm was slightly larger and the shoulder a little higher than his left one.

Richard, Duke of Gloucester, was frail and sickly in his childhood. Probably because his older brother, the King, was so mighty, strong and healthy, Richard was fiercely resolved to overcome his weakness, become strong and learn to wage war with all the ferocity and skill Edward had already shown. It may have been the rigorous training he set for himself in the use of arms that caused his slight deformity.

What did Richard of Gloucester look like? Only one portrait of him exists, painted by an unknown artist, which hangs today in Windsor Castle, showing him as King Richard III. His rather long face is a strong one, especially its jutting, determined chin. It is marked with what seem to be lines of care and worry. The eyes are not cruel, but intense and penetrating, and there is a kind of questioning look in them, as if he were trying to solve the problems and understand the evils of the Wars of the Roses, in which he took such a leading part. Only the thin-lipped, narrow mouth suggests cruelty.

There is far more character in this picture than in the exist-ing one of his brother Edward. The portrait of Edward IV is probably not a very good one. It shows a fleshy-faced man with small eyes and small, pursed mouth. Nevertheless, there is a kind of rugged strength in the face, though little to mark the amiable, easygoing, funloving king that he was.

Much happened to mould Richard's character while he was at Middleham. Along with his brother George, several other sons of nobles were at the castle, placed there under Warwick's care so that they too might benefit from the great man's knowl-edge of knightly affairs, as well as be educated in other subjects.

It was no easy kind of schooling, and much of it was rough. The boys lived and learned under a strict system. They were roused very early. They went to mass in the chapel that was part of the keep, and then had a hearty breakfast of meat, bread and ale. Classes followed in Latin, French, some law and mathematics, music, penmanship and, most important, knight-ly conduct—courtesy at all times, obedience to the rules of knighthood and a knowledge of arms, history and govern-ment.

Dinner was at about ten o'clock. Then came the rough part of the day. Clad in their small suits of armour, the boys mounted horses and galloped out over the rolling moors, fighting mock tournaments that left them with scars and bruises. They hunted the stag and wild boar and learned the difficult art of falconry. Late in the afternoon came supper, followed by playing the harp and pipes, singing and dancing. Just before they tumbled into bed the tired boys had a snack of bread and ale.

While Richard and George were learning the ways of knight-hood at Middleham, Margaret of Anjou, in Scotland with the deposed Henry VI, was seething for a chance to avenge the defeat and frightful slaughter of Towton and regain the throne for her husband. She never for a moment gave up hope, even though for the time being at least she was almost helpless.

However, she had two strong Lancastrian supporters who had survived Towton—her chief commander, Henry Beaufort, the young Duke of Somerset, and Henry Holland, Duke of Exeter. An army was raised in Scotland. The Duke of Exeter led it across the border and laid siege to the massive castle of Carlisle, which still stands there in Cumberland, the northwest corner of England.

Warwick had an able second in command to help him keep the peace in the north—his brother John Neville, who had been created Lord Montagu by the King. Montagu, with an army, hastened to the relief of Carlisle and threw the Scots back into their own country, with terrible losses.

But meanwhile, almost under Warwick's nose, another force of Scots seized three strong castles in the northeast—Bamburgh, Dunstanburgh and Alnwick. The first two stood on the coast of the North Sea; Alnwick a short distance inland. All three—Dunstanburgh in ruins—may be visited today.

The story of the three castles is the old, familiar one of treachery—not single treachery this time, not double, but triple. Warwick lost no time in bringing an army into Northumberland to recapture them. Margaret of Anjou had left Dunstanburgh and Bamburgh in command of Sir Ralph Percy, one of the famous Lancastrian family which included the Dukes of Northumberland. But Percy turned traitor, surrendered the two castles and went over to the White Rose of York. For a time Alnwick held out, but it at last surrendered.

Meanwhile, Margaret had been trying desperately to obtain more help. She had sent Henry Beaufort, Duke of Somerset, to France, where he had tried without success to get it from

King Charles VII. But in July, 1461, Charles died and was succeeded by his son, Louis XI. Buoyed by new hope, Margaret herself went to France.

Louis was a wily, unscrupulous ruler who drove a hard bargain. Yes, he would help, though his offer was not a liberal one—2,000 men, a few ships and 20,000 francs. For this he demanded the return of Calais, England's last foothold across the Channel in France. Although Calais would have to be captured from the Yorkists, Margaret agreed.

With her little army she sailed from France. She had only about eight hundred of the promised 2,000, and most of those were mercenaries she had hired, but in friendly Scotland Lancastrians who had fled there for refuge and the Scots themselves yielded enough recruits to bring Margaret's strength to about 2,000.

Warwick, who perhaps should have known better than to trust a traitor to Lancaster to remain faithful to York, had put Sir Ralph Percy in command of both Bamburgh and Dunstanburgh, which Percy had surrendered when he turned against Margaret of Anjou. As Margaret's army approached the two castles, the treacherous Percy turned traitor again. This time he betrayed the Yorkists and surrendered them to Margaret's Lancastrian army, which then headed for Alnwick.

There, more double-dealing awaited the Kingmaker. One of Warwick's trusted captains, Sir Ralph Grey, was disgruntled because the command of Alnwick had gone to Sir John Astley instead of himself. With his followers, he seized Astley, turned him over to the Queen's army and surrendered the castle to the Lancastrians. Margaret of Anjou, with three rugged castles, now had a strong foothold in northeastern England.

But bad luck dogged her. Leaving strong garrisons in the

castles, she sailed along the coast for Scotland. Four of her ships were wrecked on an island in a storm, and the crews were either captured or killed by Yorkist supporters. She herself barely escaped to Berwick, the town she had handed over to the Scots.

Margaret then decided that her best hope for more aid lay with Philip, the powerful Duke of Burgundy. She left the deposed Henry VI in Scotland and, taking her little son, the nine-year-old Prince Edward, she sailed for Flanders. "I will return with a new army," she assured her husband before she left.

Landing in Flanders, she sent a message to Philip saying she was coming to see him. The Yorkists knew of her journey, and there were English soldiers everywhere looking for her. She disguised herself as a peasant woman and rode in a cart to St. Omer, to see the Duke of Burgundy.

He welcomed her with great kindness, but he had no intention of helping her fight the Yorkists. He was secretly negotiating a peace treaty with both England and France and could not afford to help the new English government's worst enemy. But he gave her a substantial sum of money, and her father, the Duke of Anjou, gave her a home in France. She settled down there with her small son, utterly helpless to keep her promise to her husband, but grimly determined to watch and wait for a chance at another attempt on England.

VII

The Great Quarrel

Although the Lancastrians still held the three castles of
Bamburgh, Dunstanburgh and Alnwick in Northumberland,
close to the Scottish border, such power as they had was weakened. The Scots were ready to make peace with the Yorkists.
King Edward IV came to York, and there, early in 1464, a
preliminary truce was signed to last until the following October. Since the Scots were no longer his allies, the deposed
Henry VI was taken by his friends back into Northumberland
and the safety of Bamburgh Castle.

Not only did the turncoat Sir Ralph Percy, who had betrayed first the Lancastrians and then the Yorkists, come over
to the White Rose again, but so did the Lancastrian army's
commander, Henry Beaufort, Duke of Somerset. For some
reason, King Edward took a great fancy to the young duke, an
example of his too trustful nature. He gave Somerset a pardon
and gifts of money, went hunting with him and even took him
on a journey through Yorkshire on which the party's guards
were Somerset's men. Of this last, one chronicler of the time
wrote: "It was like putting wolves to guard a lamb. But God
Almighty was the shepherd."

Certainly it was a one-sided friendship. Somerset's followers had pledged his loyalty to the Yorkists in obtaining the royal pardon for him, but the duke was a Lancastrian at heart. And he had enemies. While he and the King were at Northampton some of them tried to kill the duke at Edward's own headquarters there. So the King sent him to Wales, where he would be safe.

He was safe, all right—safe to betray his benefactor. Somerset assembled a force of Lancastrians in North Wales and rode northeast, heading for Newcastle in Northumberland, where he knew he would find more supporters. It was not only a betrayal but a mistake—the costliest one of his life.

Edward, wounded to the quick by Somerset's ingratitude, learned where the duke was going. The King set out with a large force and reached Newcastle ahead of him. There he seized Somerset's supporters and executed some of them. When the duke arrived at Newcastle, its gates were shut and he had to take refuge at Bamburgh.

Sir Ralph Percy, who had turned his coat twice and was back with the Lancastrians, joined Somerset in a series of devastating raids in the northeast, burning and looting throughout the countryside. Richard Neville, Earl of Warwick, was not in the north, but his brother, John, Lord Montagu, was, and Montagu set out to destroy the two renegades. Instead, Somerset and Percy surprised him at Hedgeley Moor, not far from Alnwick, and fell upon the Yorkists fiercely. But Montagu, a masterly commander, routed them. Percy was killed in the battle, crying as he died, "I have saved the bird in my bosom." His bosom had not been a safe place for the bird, by whom he meant the deposed Henry VI.

Now only Somerset, once more among Edward IV's most

dangerous enemies, remained, since he escaped capture or death in the fight. Lord Montagu, who had gone to Newcastle, decided to put an end to this last resistance in the north. He marched out to hunt down Somerset and the remains of the Lancastrian army.

They went westward up the River Tyne, only a few miles south of the great wall across northern England that the Roman Emperor Hadrian had built in the second century. Near Hexham, on May 14, 1464, Montagu found Somerset's Lancastrian army at the Linnels, a large meadow on the south side of the Tyne.

The Lancastrians had made a bad mistake in camping there, since the place was a trap, surrounded on three sides by steep forested heights and on the fourth by the river. There was a small passage at the east end of the meadow, and there Lord Montagu promptly stationed a guard to close the trap completely. Then the main body of his army charged the Lancastrians.

Little is known of the battle or of the comparative sizes of the two forces. The Duke of Somerset's army fought with the desperation of men who know they must win or be doomed. Doom it proved to be. All were driven by Montagu's Yorkists across the river into a wood, where most of them were captured, including Somerset, who was immediately beheaded. Several other captured Lancastrian lords and a dozen or so of the deposed Henry VI's personal attendants were executed soon afterwards at Newcastle, Middleham and York.

Henry himself had been nearby, at a castle on the north side of the Tyne. His friends whisked him away to safety, but in the haste and confusion the deposed King's "bycocket"—a kind of red, turned-up, peaked cap ornamented with glittering jewels and two golden crowns—was left behind. It was found when the Yorkists ransacked the castle.

King Edward had gone to Pontefract, and there John Neville, Lord Montagu, rode to report his victory and present the trophy of the bycocket to his sovereign. Then Warwick's brother went after the three castles. Alnwick surrendered on June 23 and Dunstanburgh the next day. Meanwhile, Warwick himself, who had been in the south, had returned to the army. He led the siege against Bamburgh, which stubbornly held out. Heavy cannon were brought up, ready to pound the castle's walls. But first Warwick sent a stern demand to its Lancastrian commander, the traitorous Sir Ralph Grey, for immediate surrender.

"We will besiege this castle seven years if necessary," was the message conveyed to Grey by a herald. "For every gunshot that hurts a wall of this royal stronghold, this jewel, a Lancastrian head will fall."

Grey scornfully rejected the summons, and the big guns began to thunder. A cannonball crashed into the Lancastrian commander's headquarters, knocking him unconscious beneath a pile of rubble. The castle's garrison then surrendered it on July 10, 1464. Grey was captured, tried, condemned and beheaded on the spot. Throneless Henry VI was no longer at the castle when the siege began. He appears to have fled back to now unfriendly Scotland, where for some time he wandered, disguised as a monk and sheltered here and there by some still friendly to him.

For his deeds of valour in the north, the King created Lord Montagu Earl of Northumberland, a fitting reward for this member of the great Neville family.

The new earl's brother, Warwick, went back to London. He

had been and was to be very busy there and on the Continent for some time. Edward IV was still perfectly content to let his friend and close associate handle most of the government's affairs, especially diplomacy, at which Warwick was such a master. It was well known in England that the Kingmaker was practically the coruler of the country, and word of it had spread across the Channel. In France, King Louis XI remarked slyly: "They tell me they have two rulers in England—Monsieur de Warwick and another whose name I have forgotten."

Louis had not met Warwick personally, but he was most anxious to do so, for he was up to his neck in trouble, and his greatest hope for solving his difficulties was an alliance with England. Geographically and politically, France was a strange country at that time. In a relatively small area surrounding Paris, the French King ruled with full control. The rest of the country, far larger, was composed of a number of counties or duchies, supposed to be a part of France but actually ruled by counts and dukes who were in continual revolt against France itself. At that time both the large territory of Burgundy, which took in Flanders (now Belgium), and the duchy of Brittany, on the northwest coast, were practically independent and enemies of France.

Louis XI wanted England's help in subduing Burgundy and Brittany. Warwick was just as anxious for an alliance. It would be good for the trade and prosperity of the two countries, and he believed Burgundy and Brittany might be brought into the arrangement, thus establishing peace across the Channel. Nor did the Kingmaker forget that England might regain at least some of the territory she had controlled but lost there.

The earl thought the best way to bring about an alliance would be for King Edward IV to marry a member of the

French royal family. It was high time he was married, and Edward himself agreed with Warwick that it was. He wanted a son to succeed him on the throne. Several ladies of high degree connected in one way or another with the royal French House of Valois were suggested, but nothing came of these proposals until Bona of Savoy, sister of Louis' wife, was put forward. Warwick met her and found her lovely. He was sure that Edward IV, so fond of beautiful women, would jump at the chance to marry her.

Warwick had worked hard and long at this all-important matter. He suggested the marriage to the King.

"Give me the authority to go to France, your Grace, arrange a peace with Louis XI and sign a contract for your marriage to Bona," he pleaded.

He was overjoyed when Edward agreed that this was a good idea. Both he and the King wrote Louis saying they would meet him and the Burgundian envoys at St. Omer in Flanders in mid-August. Warwick seems to have had no doubt of Edward's sincerity, although the King had made no definite promise to wed Bona. The Kingmaker was not even suspicious when August approached and the King suggested a short delay in the parley.

"Such an important matter as my marriage should be put before the Privy Council," Edward said. "It is to meet at Reading in October. We will lay the subject before the members there, my dear Warwick."

The earl agreed. A short delay would not matter. There was no doubt that the Privy Council would approve.

Something did happen soon afterward, however, that Warwick did not like. He learned that Edward had been conducting secret negotiations with Brittany. The Kingmaker knew this could ruin all his maneuvering for an English-French alliance. But Jean de Lannoy, an envoy Louis XI had sent to England to discuss the negotiations, assured Warwick that the conferences arranged by Edward with the Bretons meant nothing. England would make no alliance either with Brittany or Burgundy against France.

Warwick was satisfied, even when the King appointed a group of representatives to hold further discussions with the Bretons. It was headed by John Tiptoff, Earl of Worcester; for the first time Warwick was not to handle a diplomatic matter for England.

In France, Louis XI was not so confident. The French King was no inspiring sight. His clothes, of the cheapest kind, looked as if they had come out of a ragbag. He had a coarse face, with a long, large Roman nose which fairly overhung the crooked mouth and loose lips. His bulky body perched on spindly legs. Looking into his deepset, hooded eyes, one must have felt that they veiled his true thoughts. Yet Louis was a man of the greatest intelligence, clever, able to match the intrigues and maneuvering of the wiliest diplomat—a man to test even Richard Neville, Earl of Warwick's skill at diplomacy. And Louis was most uneasy over what was or might be going on across the Channel.

Yet Warwick was as cocky as ever as he rode west from London up the Thames valley toward ancient Reading. He was still fully sure of himself, of the King's devoted friendship and of his own power as Edward's right-hand man, and one of England's richest.

And certainly the King did not fail to invite the Kingmaker when a group of those closest to him were assembled before the full Privy Council met there in Reading. Warwick had never seen Edward in such high spirits. He was jovial, laughing and joking, especially friendly and cordial to the earl.

The talk came around almost immediately to Louis XI. "I have great doubt of the French King's sincerity in these negotiations," said one of the King's close councillors. And he mentioned certain evidence to support his claim.

"Nonsense, my lord," snapped Warwick. "Louis is most anxious for a lasting peace between our two great nations." He looked expectantly at King Edward for support.

The King said nothing.

One of Warwick's friends, probably by previous arrangement with the earl, brought up the subject of the King's marriage. "Your subjects throughout the realm are eagerly awaiting your betrothal to the Duke of Savoy's daughter, the Lady Bona, your Grace. It is our hope that you will ally yourself with such a one as befits your high estate and will most benefit it."

"You are right, my good lord," replied the King. "We truly wish to be married." But he added something that for the first time must have sent a shiver of suspicion wriggling up Warwick's spine: "Perchance our choice may not be to the liking of all present." A smile wreathed his face as he went on: "Nevertheless, we will do as it likes us."

There was not a soul among those gathered about him who doubted for a moment that Edward would accept Bona, his trusted Warwick's choice. Of course, the King was having his little joke before he announced it.

"Whom do you wish to marry, your Grace?" one asked.

The King was still smiling genially. "I would have to wife Elizabeth Woodville, daughter of our trusty and well-beloved Lord Rivers."

There was dead silence in the chamber. Not even Warwick

replied. It was too absurd to be thought of. At last the Archbishop of Canterbury spoke meekly. "Your Grace, we doubt not the virtue and beauty of Dame Elizabeth. But so far beneath your Grace in station . . . we . . . we cannot believe this. She is no wife for a great King . . ."

"We will have her and none other," the King replied flatly.

All was not lost. Surely the King, once he had considered this foolish step, would change his mind. Earnestly they besought him to do so.

Then Edward IV exploded his bombshell—the greatest shock and humiliation of the Earl of Warwick's life.

"I have already married Elizabeth Woodville," the King announced.

It is to Warwick's great credit that he stifled his astonishment, rage and shame. Like the true noble he was, he sponsored the new Queen's presentation to the Privy Council at Reading Abbey, where all the lords formally paid her homage. But beneath the Kingmaker's calm exterior he was seething.

A few days later he received another slap in the face. The Queen's younger sister, Margaret, was betrothed to Thomas, Lord Maltravers, the son and heir of the powerful Earl of Arundel, a close associate of the King. It was enough to give Warwick cause to wonder—did Edward propose to establish a House of Woodville that would outrank that of Neville?

This was more than Warwick could bear. The safety valve which had held his temper in check popped off. He strode to the royal chambers at Westminster for a face-to-face confrontation with the King. There he hurled his rage and humiliation straight into Edward's face.

Just what was said is not known, but on the Kingmaker's part it was bitter and as sharp as the stroke of a whiplash. It covered everything—how this stupid marriage had wrecked England's political future as far as France was concerned, the King's deception of him, the ingratitude shown the man who had worked so hard and risked so much to put Edward on the throne of England, how both nobility and the common people were shocked beyond belief. All this the King had done, not only to England but to him, Richard Neville, Earl of Warwick, the Kingmaker.

Then the earl stormed from the room. He took his retainers of the Ragged Staff and a number of other outraged nobles with him and galloped north to Middleham Castle.

The great quarrel had begun.

VIII

The Kingmaker's Revenge

The King had hoodwinked not only Warwick, but everyone else of consequence in the realm. After his progress south following the victory at Towton, when he had first laid eyes on Elizabeth Woodville at Lord Rivers' manor of Grafton, Edward had visited the beautiful widow often, always in such secrecy that no one of note knew of it. He would have had a guard, of course, but every member must have known that if he breathed a word of the King's trysts he would find his head missing.

As for Lord Rivers, his daughter and the rest of the Woodville family, they knew well what they were about, and their lips were locked. They were upstarts, ambitious and greedy for power. Probably they could scarcely believe the stroke of fortune which had fallen their way. Lord Rivers was prosperous enough, but his only pretence to high rank was that his second wife, Elizabeth's mother, had been the widow of the great Duke of Bedford. Elizabeth, until the King began to pay her court, had no prospects at all, either of great wealth or of a new husband of high degree. And not only had her first husband died fighting the Yorkists, but she herself had been one of Queen Margaret of Anjou's ladies of the bedchamber.

Nevertheless, this miracle had come to pass. When Edward revealed the secret, Elizabeth had been his wife for over five months. With a few close, tight-mouthed friends, he had slipped away on April 30, 1464, under the pretence of a hunting trip. The next day, at Grafton, accompanied only by Elizabeth's mother, the former Duchess of Bedford, two of her own attendants, a priest and a boy to serve at the altar during the nuptial mass, she and King Edward IV were married.

The Woodvilles were ready to make the most of it. Their tribe was large—Elizabeth had seven sisters and five brothers, as well as a horde of relatives. Practically all profited handsomely in one way or another by the royal marriage.

One of Edward's first actions was to appoint his father-in-law an earl and give him the post of Constable of England, which made him, by title at least, commander of the royal armies. Later, the new Earl Rivers was given the even higher post of Treasurer of England.

There followed marriages galore, all designed to make the Woodvilles more powerful. In addition to that of Margaret Woodville to the Earl of Arundel's heir, the new Queen arranged for two other sisters to wed the heirs of the Earls of Essex and Kent. For another sister, Katherine, Elizabeth decreed her marriage to young Henry Stafford, who had succeeded his father, Humphrey, as Duke of Buckingham. He was only a boy; yet he was a born aristocrat, and he turned up his nose at a marriage of such low degree. But as a ward of the King he had to obey, though he hated his wife and the Woodvilles forever after. And to give her twenty-year-old brother, John Woodville, high rank, Elizabeth married him off to a

woman old enough to be his grandmother—the Dowager
Duchess of Norfolk, nearly eighty and, of all things, the aunt
of Richard Neville, Earl of Warwick.

A worse insult lay in store for the Kingmaker. The daughter
and heiress of the Duke of Exeter, who was in exile with
Margaret of Anjou, had been promised to Warwick's nephew.
Edward's Queen bribed the exiled Duke of Exeter's wife, who
was still in England and needy, to give her daughter to Elizabeth's own son by her first marriage, Thomas Grey, for a tidy
sum of money.

The brooding Warwick did not attend the Queen's coronation on May 26, 1465. He missed a great show. Elizabeth had
a stately beauty, though it was marred by her petulant mouth,
calculating expression and haughtiness toward inferiors. But
her blonde hair, sleek and shining and so long that when let
down it reached almost to her knees, was her great glory, and
she always made the most of it. She was regal in her satin,
ermine-trimmed robes as she was borne on a litter drawn by
two magnificent horses—one chestnut, one white—to Westminster Abbey. The King had showered her with jewels, and
she glittered like an overtrimmed Christmas tree.

In the great abbey the ceremony was performed by Thomas
Bourchier, Archbishop of Canterbury. There followed a great
tournament, with knights jousting for the new Queen's pleasure, and much feasting.

Meanwhile, powerful figures were trying to reconcile King
Edward and Warwick. Each needed the other badly. Even the
earl's brother George, who had become Archbishop of York, as
well as Edward's closest friend, William, Lord Hastings, used
their influence to smooth things over. And while Warwick had
not forgiven the King, he wisely bided his time and let the

reconciliation proceed. He returned to Westminster and once more took charge of diplomatic affairs, though the Woodvilles had snatched away much of his power in other directions. As for the King, he was always ready to forgive and forget an injury, and he treated Warwick as though the earl's savage reproaches had never been spoken.

There was much for the Kingmaker to do in France. The troubles that constantly simmered between King Louis XI and the rulers of Burgundy, Brittany and other provinces which were supposed to be part of Louis' kingdom but really were not were about to break out again. King Edward IV was worried, particularly over Burgundy, since England's trade with that large and powerful duchy was most valuable. He sent Warwick to France to arrange a settlement. Unfortunately, even the earl's skill failed, and the negotiations came to nothing.

Meanwhile, the pitiable one-time King Henry VI was still wandering, in his monk's disguise, about northern England, while his wife kept on with what seemed hopeless attempts to obtain aid on the Continent for an invasion of England to rescue and restore her husband to the throne. Edward IV was well aware that Henry, desperate and destitute as he was, still threatened the Yorkist rule of England. He would have to be caught and, in one way or another, made harmless. King Edward had his secret agents scouring the north country in search of the fugitive.

Once, while Henry was being sheltered by a Lancastrian friend in Yorkshire, a band of armed men burst in while he, his benefactor and several other Lancastrian followers were at dinner. The deposed King was ready to submit meekly, but one of his friends, with drawn sword, hacked a way clear for Henry to escape.

For a time he continued to wander, until July 13, 1465, when he was captured by one of King Edward's men, who tied Henry's legs together under his horse's belly and set off with his prisoner for London. Word of the capture flew ahead and reached the capital. Warwick, who had just returned from Calais, rode north to the suburb of Islington, where he met and escorted Henry to the Tower of London.

Henry was a prisoner, though he was not kept like one. He was given comfortable quarters, treated with all kindness and allowed to have all the visitors he wished. Perhaps this meek and ineffectual man, so unfitted to be a king in those times, was happier there, even though his freedom was gone, guards were always nearby and just outside rose the walls of the great fortress.

Warwick continued to play his game of forgiveness and friendship for King Edward. When Queen Elizabeth gave birth to her first child, a daughter, the earl was sponsor for the little princess at her baptism. But it must have galled him when, at the banquet which followed the ceremony, the haughty Queen dined apart from the rest in an elaborate side-chamber, not only with all her ladies-in-waiting but with her own mother kneeling there in silence while she ate.

Warwick had to do something to match this display of Woodville arrogance and show that the House of Neville was still powerful. So he gave a dinner at his town house, to which everyone of consequence was invited. It was a mammoth affair, with sixty courses served. Countless sheep, oxen, swans, egrets and other exotic birds were prepared by over fifty cooks, with many other fancy confections and pastries to go with them.

The Kingmaker then crossed the Channel again to resume his peace negotiations. He scored a notable success. A truce until March, 1468, with a peace conference that October of

1466, was signed by Louis XI, the Duke of Burgundy, and by Warwick in the name of King Edward IV. During this time Louis promised to give no aid to the Lancastrians, while the English were not to aid Burgundy in case the duke should attack France. Louis was also to pay Edward 40,000 gold crowns a year as long as the agreement lasted, and also find a high-ranking mate for Edward's sister, Margaret of York.

The King approved the agreement, but some skulduggery of which Warwick knew nothing was going on. Edward was still secretly negotiating with the dukes of Burgundy and Brittany. As the time for the peace conference with the French approached, the King did nothing about sending emissaries there.

Now Warwick began preparations for a definite move against the King. He felt confident of help from his admirer King Louis XI, but he wanted strong allies in England, and wished to undermine the Woodvilles and Edward himself in any way he could.

First, Warwick set out to win over the King's two brothers. That was not as preposterous as it sounds. Edward had become King because he was the eldest of the sons of Richard, Duke of York, who had fallen at Wakefield. Next came George, Duke of Clarence, then Richard, Duke of Gloucester, both already seen growing up at Middleham under Warwick's protection and guidance.

The earl's best prospect of bringing them to his side was that he had been so close to both of them at Middleham when they were boys. With Richard of Gloucester he failed, however. The young duke remained staunchly loyal to his brother the King.

With George of Clarence it was different. In 1466 he was seventeen years old. Even as a boy at Middleham he had been a spoiled brat, and in his teens he had not changed. He was handsome and had a smooth tongue, but he was weak-willed and not at all brilliant. The strongest force in his character was his ambition. He never forgave Edward for being born first and thus, as heir to the Duke of York, coming to the throne. Since in 1466 Clarence was next in line for it, however, he hated the Woodvilles because, if Queen Elizabeth were to have a son, his chance of ever becoming King would be small indeed. And at the royal Court in Westminster, Clarence was sulky and arrogant. He was an ideal prospect for Warwick if the earl could offer him enough in return.

Warwick baited a hook for each of the two brothers. On the first the lure was his own lovely daughter, Isabel Neville, as a wife for Clarence. The second appears to have been an excellent marriage for Gloucester, though he was only fourteen at the time.

The brothers met secretly with Warwick, who told them of the choice delicacies he was prepared to offer them. It would seem that King Edward was not sure that Warwick had forgiven him, for he learned of the meeting and was furious.

He summoned the two young men before him. "Word of your meeting with the Earl of Warwick has come to my ears," he began, and thereupon demanded abruptly: "Have either of you agreed to marry one of his daughters?"

Both of them denied it.

"I want the truth," Edward said sternly, "and the truth I will have or it will go hard with you."

And in one way or another he got it. He gave them a tongue-lashing, then said, "You will seek no marriage without my permission."

The glowering Clarence flared up. "Why not?" he cried. "If

I wish to marry Isabel Neville, why should I not do so? It is an excellent match!"

"By St. Thomas the Martyr!" roared the King, "I will punish you both in a way you will never forget if you disobey my command!"

He summoned guards into the royal chamber. "Lock these two up!" he cried. And to give them an idea of worse punishment to follow if they persisted in defying him, he kept them confined in a chamber.

Although Gloucester was lost to him, Warwick had Clarence, for the rebellious young duke was determined to marry the Kingmaker's beautiful daughter, Isabel Neville. As for the earl's own brothers, George, Archbishop of York and Chancellor of England, was his secret ally, and a valuable one. In spite of being the second highest churchman in England he was a thorough man of the world—clever, cunning, fond of intrigues and a man of great charm, though without the resolution his brother Warwick had in a crisis. But John Neville, the former Montagu, whom Edward had made Earl of Northumberland and commander of the northern army, could not be persuaded to join the conspiracy. He was strictly a military man and a brilliant one, had no use for intrigue and was loyal to the King. If Warwick could have won him over, he would have been of invaluable help.

The earl had brought another useful man to his side, however—Lord Thomas Stanley, who had so much influence in Lancashire and Cheshire, but who always made sure which way the wind was blowing before taking sides. He was a powerful though undependable ally for Warwick.

The earl also cultivated the friendship of the Earls of Oxford and Shrewsbury, and was hopeful of inducing the King's dearest friend, Lord Hastings, to come with him. Hastings, who liked to get along with everybody, was Warwick's brother-in-law.

Meanwhile, for the nobles of the Court, it was always open house at Warwick's fine town house in London. And in the House of Commons of Parliament, where the representatives of the people sat, as well as among the common people themselves, Warwick was enormously popular. Thus, still biding his time, the Kingmaker gathered strength and support for the moment when he would strike.

Meanwhile, he was still directing negotiations with Louis XI, while Edward carried on his secret ones with Louis' enemy, the Duke of Burgundy, which finally resulted in a treaty between England and the Burgundians. Warwick decided it was time for his long-awaited personal meeting with Louis. In May, 1467, he set out from London with a retinue that would have done credit to any foreign prince visiting a powerful king.

Before Warwick arrived in France, Louis had a talk with Margaret of Anjou's brother, the Duke of Calabria, an Italian province.

"Why, if you are so fond of this traitor to the English King, do you not enlist his aid in helping my sister Margaret regain the throne for her husband, the rightful King of the English?" asked the Italian duke. "Then you would be certain of English friendship. The usurper Edward makes treaties with your enemies behind your back."

The crafty Louis XI gave the duke's proposal some serious thought. Was a reconciliation between Warwick and Margaret of Anjou really possible? The French King was well aware of the long-standing hatred between them. Warwick had called Henry VI's Queen an unprintable name. And it was this man, whom the English called the Kingmaker, who had put Edward IV on the throne in place of Henry VI. Yet Louis knew how deep were the wounds in Warwick's heart for the treatment Edward had given him, how the earl despised the Woodvilles, who had robbed him of so much influence, and, above all, Warwick's consuming ambition for power. It just might work.

Louis mounted his horse and rode out to meet Warwick. When they met at a small village, Louis greeted him like a long-lost brother, caressed him and treated him as though he, not Edward, were King of England. They rode on together to Rouen, and there also Warwick was feted and entertained in royal fashion, and hospitality lavished on all his entourage.

While the emissaries in Warwick's party negotiated with the French diplomats, Louis and the earl talked intimately. When Warwick at last burst out with all the pent-up injury that was in his heart, his cunning host began to feel that his guest could be persuaded to make peace with Margaret of Anjou and come to her aid.

A treaty had been drawn up. What England wanted most was to recover some of her lost French territory. Louis made this concession in return for an English-French alliance against Burgundy: he would let the Pope in Rome decide whether the rich duchies of Normandy and Guienne rightfully belonged to England. And again there was the promise of a substantial payment to Edward IV and a suitable husband for the King's sister.

"But suppose, my dear friend, that King Edward rejects our generous offer?" Louis asked.

Warwick drew himself up to his full height. "I have authority," he said, "and I shall use it, come what will."

"I know the vast power you have in England," murmured the artful Frenchman, "but would it not be better if he who rules England only because you, good Warwick, placed him upon the throne there, were—ah—shall we say, unable to use *his* authority? If the rightful King, the deposed Henry VI, were restored—he is not a man of strong will—you could be certain of controlling him."

"How would you propose to accomplish this, your Grace?"

"It would be quite simple, my dear Warwick. The House of Lancaster would gladly accept your aid, nor would it forget you once it returns to power. By chance it happens that an emissary of Queen Margaret is at my Court this very moment."

Warwick frowned. "It pleasures me not to aid this woman."

Louis had another card up his sleeve in this game of intrigue. "Let us suppose," he began, "that my rebellious liege, the Duke of Burgundy, were exterminated and the rule of his great duchy fell vacant. It would then be in my power to create a prince to rule part of it—say, perhaps, Holland and Zeeland. A man like yourself, so well fitted for a princedom."

A gratified smile wreathed Warwick's face. This he liked. To be a European prince with a rich domain.

"I shall consider what you have said, your Grace," he said. "Meanwhile, let the proposed treaty be submitted by your emissaries at Westminster. I am empowered to sign it, but it will be better for our purposes if it is laid before the King."

With that, Warwick returned to England. Another shock awaited him there. While he had been away, King Edward had ridden to the Archbishop of York's palace near Charing Cross, just outside the walls of the City of London. There he confronted Warwick's brother, George Neville, the archbishop, with a demand that he surrender the Great Seal of his office as Chancellor of England. The King waited until it was put in his hands, then rode back to Westminster. A few days later he gave the high post to Robert Stillington, Bishop of Bath and

Wells, whom Edward trusted as his loyal supporter. Another Neville had fallen from power.

Warwick's rage at this became even greater when the French envoys arrived in England for the signing of the treaty. They received a cool welcome, none from King Edward. When Warwick talked with them he was well aware that the ouster of his brother George Neville meant that Edward had chosen an alliance with Burgundy rather than France.

"Did you see those about the King?" the earl stormed.

"Do not heat yourself, my lord," said the Admiral of France, who was among Louis XI's emissaries. "You will be avenged."

"Know ye," Warwick raged, "that these are men by whom my brother has been dismissed as Chancellor of England!" He meant the Woodvilles.

After six weeks the French delegates went home, the treaty unsigned. Duke Philip of Burgundy having died while Warwick was still in France, Edward IV resumed the treaty of friendship with the new duke, Philip's son Charles. Warwick went back to Yorkshire, fuming. His brother George soon joined him at Middleham. There, Warwick's followers began to assemble.

The split between the earl and the King was now open, wide and widening. Edward heard a report that Margaret of Anjou was back in Warwick's favour. He commanded the earl to appear at Westminster and explain. Warwick returned an angry refusal.

Edward badly needed the Kingmaker's friendship and talents once more. Things were not going well for the King. Plans had been made to marry his sister Margaret of York to young Charles of Burgundy, but the new duke kept putting it off and making exorbitant demands for trade concessions first. Edward yielded and revoked decrees barring imports from Burgundy. It meant that exports of Burgundian goods would come flooding in, competing with English manufactures, and this won the King much ill will.

All over the kingdom the people were disgruntled. They blamed the Woodvilles for their troubles. On New Year's Day, 1468, a Kentish mob attacked the estate of Richard Woodville, Lord Rivers, and ravaged it, though the servants whisked away his valuables to a safe hiding place.

The King was even worried about his own safety. But Coventry remained strongly loyal, and there the King went to spend Christmas. He was still there early in January, 1468, when he sent a curt command to Warwick to join him there. The earl replied with an equally terse demand: let the Woodvilles and another enemy, Lord Herbert, appointed Earl of Pembroke in place of the exiled Jasper Tudor, be dismissed from the Court, and he would come.

Warwick's brother George, in spite of what the King had done to him, wanted to make peace if possible, probably thinking thus to regain his lost chancellorship. He had a secret meeting with Earl Rivers, and Warwick then learned that if he would come to Coventry he would be received with all the honour befitting his allegiance. He did come, and the Woodvilles were kept out of the way. He accepted a reconciliation with Lord Herbert and others of his enemies at Court, and the King and his council received him most cordially.

But it was all a hollow sham. One reason the King wanted to see Warwick was to borrow money to pay the large sum his sister Margaret needed as dowry for her marriage to Duke Charles of Burgundy. Edward also asked the earl to raise 4,000 archers Duke Francis of Brittany wanted to defend his duchy against an invasion by Louis XI. Warwick refused both requests.

Nevertheless, he did lead Margaret of York's great escort of lords and ladies when she started for the coast to sail for Burgundy and her wedding. At a halt en route there was an elaborate feast at which Warwick mingled not only with the Dukes of Clarence and Gloucester, but also with the Woodvilles. It was all a part of his cat-and-mouse game. Let the King think all was well.

Early in 1469 Edward must have been convinced of it; the earl seemed to be his old self, using all his charm and radiating goodwill upon the King, who rewarded him with a number of estates to add to his already vast holdings. But Warwick was in command of the English navy in the Channel, a dangerous threat to the King.

Edward did not know that Warwick had already prepared a plan of action. It was to come from two directions—from the south by an army led by Warwick himself, and from the north by one commanded by a mysterious figure, Robin of Redesdale.

Robin had assembled a force of Lancastrian sympathizers in Yorkshire and Lancashire. He had orders from Warwick: he was to wait for word to march southward. And to both Robin and his leaders in the south, the earl made it plain that this was to be no mob attack. It must be made by trained armies.

Early in May, 1469, Warwick, who had been at Calais, crossed the Channel to Sandwich. There his flagship, the *Trinity,* was being rebuilt and fitted out, along with other warships. By the end of the month thirty of them were patrolling the Channel, with more being readied for sea in case Duke Charles of Burgundy should try to keep his promise of aid to England.

Meanwhile, the whole venture nearly came to disaster. Robin of Redesdale's men, eager for action, rose too early in the north. Warwick's brother, John Neville, Earl of Northumberland, intercepted and routed them. But Robin escaped and reassembled his force, which had fled.

Warwick finally sent the long-awaited order. He was at Windsor with the King, who was blissfully unconscious of what was being planned. But learning of Robin of Redesdale's and other smaller uprisings in the north, Edward decided to investigate. The troubles there did not worry him much; the staunch Earl of Northumberland was there, and Warwick was once more loyal. So he thought. Thus he took only a small force with him and his northward journey was a leisurely one.

Warwick went back to Sandwich. There men, weapons and armour were flooding in. Red-jacketed men wearing the Ragged Staff were everywhere. And far to the north, Robin of Redesdale, with between 5,000 and 6,000 men, was making his way southward.

On his journey the King stopped at a manor that George Neville, still Archbishop of York, owned in Hertfordshire. He suggested that George come with him to Yorkshire, where his influence as archbishop would be helpful in quieting the people. Geroge said he had a small matter to attend to first, but would come along soon. He came along, all right, but not as the King expected.

The moment Edward and his force left, George made all speed south to Sandwich. Warwick, Clarence and Isabel were there. They slipped across the Channel to Calais, and there, on June 11, the archbishop married them. Now, it seemed, Warwick could be sure of Clarence's loyalty.

Back across the Channel, Warwick took command of his army, now on the Lancastrian side, and marched for London.

He was given a tumultuous welcome by the people, though the mayor and aldermen were merely polite, for they were worried. But Warwick told them that he and Clarence were marching to join the King, and with that the city fathers loaned the earl £1,000, though he did not offer much security for the money.

By this time the King had learned Warwick's secret, well kept for so long. He halted at Nottingham and waited there, apparently because he had received word that a force of Welsh pikemen under Lord Herbert, the new Earl of Pembroke, and archers from the west country commanded by Humphrey Stafford—whom Edward IV had created the Earl of Devon in place of the Lancastrian, John Courtenay—were marching to his aid.

Warwick appears to have learned of this also. He sent a mounted force coursing ahead to reinforce Robin of Redesdale's men. It headed for Banbury in the Oxfordshire Midlands on the route the Earls of Pembroke and Devon would be taking. The Kingmaker and his main army followed.

The King's western Yorkist followers reached Banbury first. There the Earls of Pembroke and Devon quarrelled over a trifling matter. In a huff, Devon drew his archers back ten miles from Banbury. The dispute was disastrous, not only for Pembroke and Devon but above all for Edward IV. On July 26, 1469, at Edgecot, near Banbury, Robin of Redesdale and his Lancastrian army discovered and fell upon the Earl of Pembroke's Yorkist pikemen with savage fury. The Welshmen put up a fierce resistance with their murderous weapons, but without archers they were doomed.

The outcome of the battle depended upon a race between the archers Devon sent to join Pembroke and Warwick's advance horsemen. The Kingmaker's riders got there first. They charged onto the field, making Edward's Yorkist followers from the west believe that it was the earl's own main army by raising the shout of "A Warwick! A Warwick!" which so terrified them that they fled in disorder. Meanwhile, the King and his army were on the way from Nottingham. But word of the disaster at Edgecot (it is generally called the battle of Banbury) reached them, and most of the King's men deserted.

Edward IV was now helpless. Warwick learned that he was at Olney, about thirty miles to the east. The earl did not want it to appear that he was seizing the King by force, and he sent his brother George Neville, the archbishop, to Olney in his place. George found the King with only a small escort, which included Richard, Duke of Gloucester, and Lord Hastings.

"Your Grace, may I humbly suggest that you permit yourself to be escorted to your faithful lieges, the Earl of Warwick and your brother, the Duke of Clarence?" the archbishop asked.

The King knew perfectly well that this was no invitation to a friendly gathering over a tankard of wine, but he amiably agreed to go along.

Richard Woodville, Earl Rivers, and his son, Sir John Woodville, had fled, but they were captured along the Severn River about two weeks later and executed. So was the Yorkist Earl of Devon, taken by a mob in Somerset and slain.

Just what happened when the King and Warwick met is not known, but the meeting appears to have been friendly. Nevertheless, with Edward IV in his hands, Warwick was taking no chances on losing him. Within a day or two Edward was safely behind the strong walls of Warwick Castle.

The Kingmaker was avenged. Edward IV was his prisoner. Now the question was: what was Warwick going to do with him?

IX

The Kingmaker Restores a King

True, Richard Neville, Earl of Warwick, was avenged, but he soon found it a hollow triumph. Although Edward IV was his prisoner, he was still King of England. And there was not much the earl could do about it.

One answer to his problem—and he probably considered it —was a bad one indeed. It was in his power to kill Edward and install George, Duke of Clarence, next in line for the throne, as King. But it would not work, and Warwick knew it. For one thing, he knew enough by that time about Clarence's character—shallow, mean and lacking intelligence—to realize that Edward's next younger brother would not be a good ruler for England nor one he himself could trust.

Besides, while it was true that before the Kingmaker's successful rebellion the English people were dissatisfied, their discontent was with the Woodvilles, whom they blamed for all the trouble. Now their power was shattered, with Richard Woodville, Earl Rivers, and his son, Sir John Woodville, dead. The only ones of any consequence left of the numerous tribe were Rivers' eldest son, Anthony, the former Lord Scales, who had now succeeded to his father's title, and Queen Elizabeth. As for the rest, and their supporters who held high posts in the government, Warwick lost no time in replacing them with his own followers.

Thus, with the menace of the Woodvilles broken, the people wanted their King to remain on the throne, and Edward IV knew it. Now it was his turn to play a waiting game.

After depositing the King at Warwick Castle, the Kingmaker had gone to London. The City was in a chaos of fear and unrest. There were demands that the King be released. And since there was little law and order, London was close to anarchy, and many greedy men took advantage of it to seize what they wanted for themselves.

There was a menacing threat from across the Channel too. The Duke of Burgundy, Edward IV's ally and new husband of the King's sister, sent a promise of aid for London if the city remained loyal to Edward; if it did not, he would take vengeance upon it.

Warwick had summoned Parliament to meet at York in September, 1469, to give him some sort of authority to govern. But he feared that if it met it would turn against him, and he cancelled the session. He also decided that the King was too near London. Edward was secretly moved from Warwick Castle to Yorkshire, travelling only by night, to Middleham. There, on the lonely moors, he would be safer from rescue.

England still clamored for its King. There were riots and devastating raids all over the country in which many people were slain and churches and houses pillaged. Something had to be done. Warwick sent his brother, George Neville, to Middleham.

"Your faithful liege, the Earl of Warwick, wants the people

to know you are still their King," the archbishop told Edward. "He desires only to know what course you will take, your Grace, if you are given your liberty."

"I hold no ill will against the Nevilles," replied the King amiably. "You may tell my friend and liege, the earl, that I shall seek no retaliation."

"Then if you will accompany me to York, you will enter the city in royal state before all the people, and you may then take up your residence at Pontefract Castle."

The King understood Warwick's strategy perfectly—a gesture to keep him and the people satisfied while the Kingmaker struggled to hold the power he had regained. He agreed to the arrangement, knowing he had the earl right where he wanted him.

Edward still had many friends among the great lords. After his splendid entrance into York and his journey to Pontefract, he summoned them to the brooding Yorkshire stronghold. Richard, Duke of Gloucester, and Lord Hastings rode in with a force of armed men. The Duke of Buckingham, the Earls of Arundel and Essex and other lords came with their retainers. So did loyal John Neville, Earl of Northumberland, Warwick's brother. When about a thousand men were gathered at Pontefract, Edward nonchalantly sent word to Warwick that he was coming to London. The earl could do nothing to prevent it. He and the Duke of Clarence left London. For some weeks they appear to have roamed the Midlands and north country in a desperate attempt to keep a hold on the kingdom outside London.

Edward was back again in the full power of his sovereignty. He dismissed those Warwick had appointed to high offices and replaced them with his followers. His loyal brother, the Duke of Gloucester, became Constable of England. A Woodville, Anthony, the new Earl Rivers, was at Court.

Yet the King longed for the old days when Warwick had taken the burden of rule and diplomacy off his shoulders. He wanted very much to return to the pleasures he loved too well —hunting, feasting, drinking and the society of beautiful ladies. He sent his brother, the Duke of Clarence, and Warwick an invitation to attend a Great Council at Westminster. It appeared to be a peace gesture, but the Kingmaker did not fully trust the King and demanded full guarantees of safety before coming. These were given, and Warwick and Clarence set out for London.

Warwick was still not completely reassured. He and Clarence took along a powerful force of Red Jackets, fully armed. They were not needed, however.

The reconciliation at Westminster was much like the previous one. Warwick, Clarence and their followers were given royal pardons. The grievances of both sides were to be forgotten. Finally, the King made what he seemed to think was a grand gesture. He betrothed his daughter Elizabeth (she was three years old!) to George Neville and created him Duke of Bedford. This was not Archbishop George Neville, of course, but the son of John Neville, Earl of Northumberland, who had never wavered in his loyalty to the King. One wonders what Warwick thought of this empty apple-polishing.

In truth, it was anything but a conciliation. Publicly, the King spoke of Warwick and his brother the archbishop, and of his own brother, George, Duke of Clarence, as his "best friends." But he was probably not surprised when he discovered a little later that the earl and Clarence had gone right on intriguing against him.

The two conspirators succeeded in stirring up one serious uprising. Some of their Lancastrian supporters raised a force in the north to oppose the King, who got word that trouble was brewing and marched in that direction. He surprised the rebels near Stamford on the southern Lincolnshire border. Nevertheless, the Lancastrian commander, Sir Robert Welles, tried to rally them and intimidate the royal army, as had happened at Edgecot, by raising a cry of "A Warwick! A Clarence!" but it did not work. As Welles's men fled, many threw away their chain-mail jackets to run faster, and the rout became known as the battle of Lose-Coat Field.

Edward got his hands on some of those who had plotted the revolt and beheaded them. As for Warwick and Clarence, both in the conspiracy up to their necks, the best the King could do was to declare them traitors. That made England too hot for them. With their wives and Warwick's daughter Anne, they raced for the coast of Devonshire, with the King and Richard, Duke of Gloucester, in hot pursuit. The two master plotters managed to find a ship to take them across the Channel. They landed at Honfleur in Normandy, where representatives of Louis XI gave them a royal welcome.

There was one hope left to Warwick—aid from Louis. Early in that June of 1470 he met the French King at Amboise. The earl offered to help Margaret of Anjou restore Henry VI to the throne in return for Louis' aid. But such was the hatred that had existed for years between Warwick and Margaret that only Louis could bring enough pressure upon her so that she would even consider a reconciliation.

The French King and the earl discussed the subject at great length. "It will not be easy," Louis warned. "Margaret of Anjou will insist upon being sure of your allegiance."

"That can be arranged," replied Warwick. "I shall propose

to her a marriage between my second daughter, the Lady Anne, and Margaret's son Edward, the rightful Prince of Wales."

"Ah," said Louis, "we shall have to see whether Margaret of Anjou will accept such an offer. But there is another problem to be settled. We propose to restore Henry VI, the rightful King of England, to his throne. In that case the crown would go to young Edward upon Henry's death. But what of your friend and ally, the Duke of Clarence? Will he not expect that as Edward IV's next younger brother, the crown should come to him?"

Warwick sat for some time deep in thought. Louis was right; Clarence would surely raise a terrible turmoil over the succession to the throne. He had formed his alliance with Warwick with the idea of becoming King. And he had the rank and friends to make plenty of trouble for Warwick, Louis and Margaret of Anjou.

At last the Kingmaker gave an expressive shrug. "I will take care of that," he said.

"But how, my dear Warwick?"

"At the moment I do not know." The earl's jaw set firmly. "But it will be done in one way or another, your Grace."

Louis communicated Warwick's proposal to Margaret of Anjou, then conferred once more with the earl.

"Margaret accepts your proposal," said Louis. He sighed. "I assure you, my good friend, it was not easy. At first she refused even to consider it. But the restoration of her husband is first in her desires. However, she makes one more demand: you must go to her at Angers in Anjou, apologize in all humility for the insults you have offered her and swear eternal allegiance to her and the House of Lancaster."

That Warwick agreed to demean himself before this Queen

in exile whom he had hated with his whole being shows that his anger against his former friend, Edward IV, was even deeper. Only the hope of completing his vengeance upon the King could have persuaded him to do so.

He went with Louis to Angers, leaving Clarence in Normandy. Margaret of Anjou could be as haughty, even in her desperation, as Edward IV's Queen, Elizabeth. She kept Warwick on his knees, apologizing for the things he had said of her, for fifteen minutes. What this must have cost the proud Warwick can only be imagined.

At last Margaret said, "I consent to the proposal. My son shall be betrothed to your daughter. But mark you, Warwick, the marriage shall not be held until my husband sits once more on the throne of England."

Margaret and Warwick then swore on a piece of the True Cross that they would be mutual allies, while Louis promised his aid to the House of Lancaster. And with that, on July 25, 1470, in the cathedral of Angers, Prince Edward, who was sixteen, and the Lady Anne Neville, fourteen, were officially betrothed.

As for George, Duke of Clarence, Warwick brought back to Normandy one small concession: if Prince Edward and Anne should have no sons, the crown should pass to Clarence upon young Edward's death. It was the slimmest of hopes for him, but he accepted it. No doubt plots to change all that were already simmering in his not too agile mind.

It took only about a month to assemble the ships and troops for the invasion. The fleet, provided by Louis, sailed across the Channel. Luck was with them, for a blockade of English and Burgundian warships was scattered by a providential storm, and the French vessels sailed across unmolested. The soldiers were landed on the Devonshire coast, some at Plymouth, the rest at Dartmouth.

Edward IV is said to have had supreme contempt for Warwick's military ability, and he certainly acted that way. He was fully aware of what Warwick was up to in France, and he did not take prompt action against two of the earl's allies. Warwick's brother, George Neville, the archbishop, was held a prisoner at his own manor of Moor Park in Hertfordshire. Another supporter, the Earl of Oxford, barely managed to escape to France.

But Warwick hoodwinked the King by a clever ruse. One of his adherents in the north, Lord Fitzhugh, stirred an uprising there that induced the King to march and subdue it by driving Fitzhugh and his rebels across the Scottish border. Then the King came south, but only as far as York, where he remained for some time instead of hastening on to meet the threat of an invasion by Warwick.

That was one mistake; though he had no way of knowing it, he made another, fatal one. Setting out again, he had so little regard for the possibility that Warwick could really invade that he left most of his army at Pontefract. But when he halted for the night at Doncaster, he received news of Warwick's landing. He sent couriers back to Pontefract to summon the 3,000 Yorkists he had left there. That night something happened that would be unbelievable save for something else which had taken place not long before.

Until the battle of Towton, the powerful Lancastrian Percy family had for many years been earls of Northumberland. But at Towton Henry Percy, the third earl and commander of Queen Margaret's army, had been slain. Edward had replaced him with John Neville. The King became convinced, however, that a Percy, since the family were natives of that northernmost shire of England, could more easily control its wild, fierce and unruly people. So he had replaced faithful John Neville as earl by Henry Percy, son of the one killed at Towton. He had created Neville Marquess of Montagu, a higher title, but Warwick's brother resented it deeply, nonetheless.

The deposed John Neville, once more called Montagu, marched with the 3,000 men from Pontefract upon receiving the King's summons. He joined Edward at Doncaster, but in a most unexpected way. After the King had gone to bed, one of his men burst into his chamber.

"Enemies are coming for to take you, your Grace!" the man shouted.

The enemies were Montagu and his men. The indignant marquess had at last come over to his brother Warwick's side. If Edward IV stayed at Doncaster he was trapped, with a far smaller force to fight Montagu. He, Richard of Gloucester, Lord Hastings and the young Earl Rivers leaped to their horses and galloped madly eastward.

They reached The Wash, a large, shallow bay on the coast of Norfolk and Lincolnshire. They crossed it to Lynn, on the south shore, in spite of a storm which nearly capsized their small boats and drowned them all. There they obtained some larger fishing vessels and on October 2, 1470, sailed across the North Sea to friendly Burgundy.

Warwick, the Duke of Clarence and their Lancastrian army advanced across England to London. Although the city officials and merchants supported Edward IV, the people loved the man whose troops marched under the banner of the Bear and Ragged Staff. A mob gathered, not only to welcome them but to take advantage of the disorder the invaders had caused to plunder the city, letting the prisoners out of the jails to help them. Edward IV's Queen, Elizabeth, and her two daughters were in the Tower, but they escaped to Westminster, with its religious sanctuary, where none dared molest them. Other officials of Edward's government did the same.

Warwick and his men quickly restored order in the city. Then the wretched Henry VI was rescued from his gloomy, barred room in the Tower and taken to the palace of the Bishop of London. Warwick restored his brother George, the archbishop, as chancellor, and replaced other high officials of Edward's government with his own followers. Of Edward's supporters whom he captured he executed only one—a cruel man, John Tiptoft, Earl of Worcester.

On October 13, Henry VI rode in magnificent state, first to St. Paul's, where he gave thanks to God for his restoration, then to Westminster. Meanwhile, Warwick had summoned Parliament, which met two days later. It declared Edward IV a traitor and usurper, and set the crown back on the head of Henry VI.

The vengeance of Richard Neville, Earl of Warwick, now seemed complete. The Kingmaker had lived up to his nickname by making Henry VI King once more. But again the quotation from Shakespeare, "Uneasy lies the head that wears a crown," is an apt one.

X

Warwick—the End of the Line

Richard Neville, Earl of Warwick, in his triumph, again faced the problem of holding on to what he had gained. Henry VI was back on the throne, but it was as unsteady a seat as if it had been made of cigar-box wood. Henry himself was spoken of as a "shadow on the wall," "mute as a crowned calf" and "like a sack of wool." And while Edward IV was an exile, he was as determined to be King again as Warwick had been to unseat him.

The Kingmaker, uncrowned ruler of England, was having many troubles. He had expected Queen Margaret and young Edward, Prince of Wales and heir-apparent to Henry VI's throne, to come back to England. If the people could see Margaret, and especially the young prince, it would surely bring many doubtful ones over to the side of Lancaster. But she did not come, probably as anxious as a mother hen with one chick to see that no harm came to her son, her great hope for keeping the House of Lancaster's rule of England.

Meanwhile, an event of the greatest importance took place. In her sanctuary of Westminster Abbey, Queen Elizabeth, after

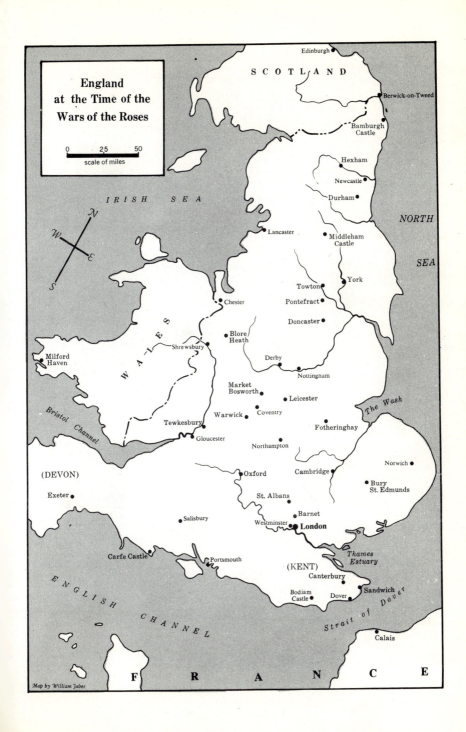

England
at the Time of the
Wars of the Roses

0   25   50
scale of miles

SCOTLAND

Edinburgh

Berwick-on-Tweed

Bamburgh
Castle

Hexham

Newcastle

Durham

IRISH   SEA

NORTH

SEA

Lancaster

Middleham
Castle

Towton

York

Chester

Pontefract

Doncaster

WALES

Blore
Heath

Shrewsbury

Derby

Nottingham

Market
Bosworth

Leicester

Warwick

Coventry

Tewkesbury

Fotheringhay

Gloucester

Northampton

The Wash

Norwich

(DEVON)

Oxford

Cambridge

Exeter

St. Albans

Bury
St. Edmunds

Barnet

Salisbury

Westminster   London

Bristol Channel

Milford
Haven

Carfe Castle

Portsmouth

Thames
Estuary

(KENT)

Canterbury

Bodium
Castle

Dover

Sandwich

ENGLISH

CHANNEL

Strait of Dover

Calais

F   R   A   N   C   E

Map by William Jaber

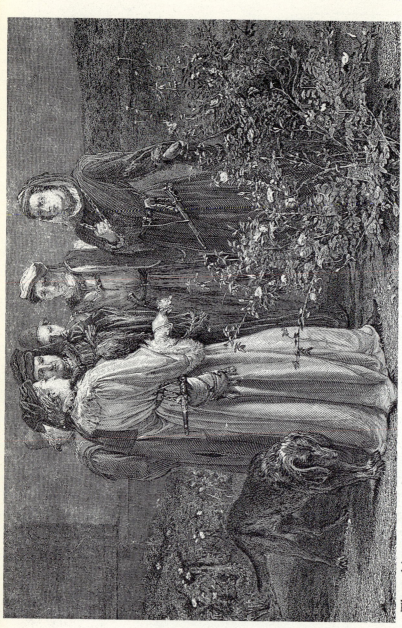

The white rose was the symbol of the House of York (but the red rose did not come to be used for the symbol of the House of Lancaster until after the crowning of Henry VII).

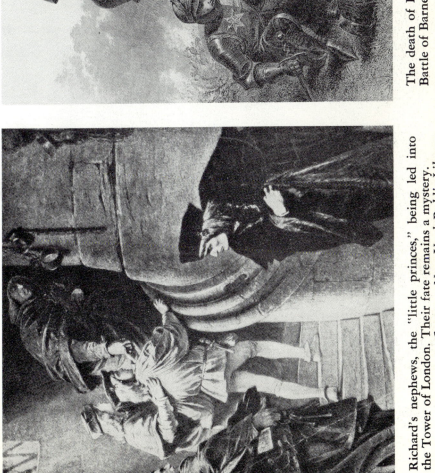

The death of Richard Nelville, Earl of Warwick, at the Battle of Barnet. *Courtesy New York Public Library*

Richard's nephews, the "little princes," being led into the Tower of London. Their fate remains a mystery. *Courtesy New York Public Library*

Henry VII being crowned after the battle at Bosworth Field in 1485.
Courtesy New York Public Library

having had two daughters, bore a son who was named Edward after his father. Edward IV, if he could regain the throne, now had an heir to succeed him.

Another of Warwick's troubles was that, much as he disliked Edward IV's brother, George, Duke of Clarence, he needed the duke's influence and help. And Clarence's mother, the Dowager Duchess of York, was striving mightily to get him to desert his father-in-law, Warwick, and return to the White Rose of York.

Also threatening Warwick was Edward IV's possible return from exile. True, the deposed King was having no easy time in obtaining Burgundy's aid for an invasion of England. Duke Charles of Burgundy was playing an artful game. Now that the House of Lancaster had triumphed, he hoped for an alliance with the new English government. He did not even welcome Edward and his youngest brother, Richard, Duke of Gloucester, personally as his guests; they stayed at the house of a friendly Burgundian noble.

But when Duke Charles learned of the agreement between Louis, Margaret and Warwick, followed by the French King's abrupt declaration of war on Burgundy, he changed his mind. A week after Christmas, 1470, he welcomed Edward and Gloucester in an audience.

Charles loaned Edward 50,000 crowns to hire ships and some Flemish troops. By early March, 1471, Edward had about 1,500 men, including a thousand of his English supporters who were in refuge with him. The fleet of nearly a score of ships sailed on March 11. Off the coast of Norfolk, a landing party was sent ashore to see what the people's feelings were. It was promptly driven back.

Edward decided to try a landing farther north. Yorkshire's

long, wild coast was less likely to be well guarded. He went ashore at Ravenspur at the mouth of the Humber River and marched to York. The gates of the old city were closed to the invaders. But Edward shouted: "Know ye that I come only to reclaim my rightful dukedom of York [his heritage as the eldest son of Richard, Duke of York, slain at Wakefield] and to support King Henry as his loyal subject." It was a lie, but it gained the army admittance to the city.

In London, Warwick learned of Edward's landing and sent a messenger galloping north to Pontefract with orders to his brother John (who had come over to the side of Lancaster when Edward took away his title of Earl of Northumberland and made him Marquess of Montagu), to stop the invaders. But John Neville disobeyed the order. There are those who say the message never reached him, others that the treacherous Duke of Clarence had also sent him orders to let Edward pass. Still others claim that in spite of his break with Edward, the old loyalty and affection remained, and he could not bring himself to destroy the deposed King and his army. Another reason given is that John Neville of Montagu did not have enough men at Pontefract to meet the invaders, though this seems strange in view of the small force that Edward had.

At any rate, Edward's Yorkist army slipped past Pontefract unmolested. He had plenty of friends on the road ahead. On his southbound march toward London he picked up archers and men-at-arms to swell his army to greater strength. Two knights brought six hundred men, while Sir William Stanley came with a host of 3,000.

Warwick had not been idle, however. He sent George, Duke of Clarence, into the southwest to gather men. The Earl of Oxford was coming from the east with a strong force. John

Neville, Marquess of Montagu, was at last marching south
from Pontefract, though slowly, with little enthusiasm. The
Kingmaker brought his own men of the Ragged Staff to
Coventry, where all were to assemble.

When Edward reached Nottingham he learned that the Lancastrian Earl of Oxford and his men were at Newark-on-Trent,
about eighteen miles to the northeast. He showed his expert
generalship by making a feint in that direction which caused
Oxford to retreat. Then Edward swung about and marched
with all speed to Leicester, where over 2,500 men joined him,
then on to Coventry.

Warwick, still waiting for his reinforcements to arrive, had
shut himself inside the walls of Coventry. On March 29, to
his dismay, he looked out upon Edward's army, massed outside
the town.

A herald rode up to the main gate with a challenge to Warwick to come out and fight. The Kingmaker refused. He was
safe enough in the town, but he may have been a little uneasy
about the Duke of Clarence's 4,000 reinforcements, reported
nearing Coventry. What with Clarence married to his daughter
and the duke's dislike of his brother Edward, he should be loyal
to Lancaster—but Warwick also knew Clarence's character.

Edward was even better acquainted with his brother's character—so well that he withdrew his army about three miles
south of Coventry. Then, with Richard, Duke of Gloucester, at
his side, he rode boldly forward to meet Clarence. Clarence too,
with only an escort of a few followers, also advanced ahead of
his force. He dismounted and fell to his knees. Edward also
dismounted, raised his younger brother up and kissed him.
Thus did the traitorous George, Duke of Clarence, betray his
father-in-law, Warwick.

The next day Edward allowed Clarence to go through the mockery of showing some remorse by going up to the walls of Coventry and offering Warwick a pardon if he would submit. The earl spurned the offer with fury.

Edward then marched for London. He reached St. Albans on April 10 and sent orders ahead to the London authorities to arrest and imprison Henry VI. They obeyed him well; not only Henry but every Lancastrian leader in the city who was unable to reach sanctuary in Westminster was clapped into prison.

Then, on April 11, 1471, Edward and Gloucester, riding at the head of their army, entered London in great splendour, with their trumpets blaring in a way that threatened to topple the city's walls as those of Joshua's army did the walls of Jericho in the Old Testament. The merchants of the city had always favoured Edward, and as for the common people, much as they loved Warwick and his Ragged Staff, few if any believed he could possibly defeat Edward in a battle, and they gave the Yorkist invader a welcome.

Edward went first to St. Paul's to give thanks to God for his restoration, then to Westminster Abbey, where the Archbishop of Canterbury set the crown of England on his head once more. This time the Kingmaker, now his enemy, had not put him on the throne. Queen Elizabeth and her children returned from their sanctuary. Edward IV, again King of England, saw his son for the first time.

However, his throne was not yet safe. In spite of his loss of the traitorous Clarence's army, Warwick had a large Lancastrian force collected at Coventry—the estimates differ, but it was probably about 12,000 men. In King Edward's case, again the estimates vary, but he is believed to have had a smaller army, about 9,000. Nevertheless, in addition to his objective of reaching London to be recrowned, his march had been designed to draw Warwick out of Coventry and meet him in one last battle which would decide the fate of one or the other forever. Edward had supreme confidence that his superiority over Warwick as a general would bring him victory.

There was not a moment to be lost. Strong rumours—they were true—had it that Margaret of Anjou had assembled an army and was about to sail and invade England. Edward IV knew Warwick must be dealt with before she could arrive and give the earl overwhelming support.

On April 13, 1471, the day before Easter, King Edward, in full armour, led his army into St. John's Fields. An enormous crowd had collected there, and the King addressed them, praising them for their loyalty. He also gave a royal pardon to all who had been forced in any way to give aid and comfort to his enemies.

Edward had released Henry VI from his cell and brought the once more deposed King with him. If anything was needed to show the people Edward's superiority over this rival for the throne, it was the pitiable sight of Henry, mounted but slumped in his saddle, a perfect picture of weakness and helplessness. Besides, Edward had wisely decided to keep Henry in his own hands, rather than leave him in London.

Then, with his Queen and her children safely lodged in the Tower, well guarded by armed men, Edward IV, having learned that Warwick had set out from Coventry and reached St. Albans, marched northwestward with his army toward Barnet. This town, less than ten miles southeast of St. Albans, is today on the very fringe of London; the end of one long spur of the underground, the London subway, is at High Barnet, just outside Barnet itself. In 1471 Barnet was well beyond the metropolis.

Along the line of march, Edward's advance guard of Yorkists encountered a patrol of Warwick's Lancastrians and drove them back. Edward had marched from London in the late afternoon, and the sun was setting. The Yorkist army had to take up its position in darkness to be ready for battle in the morning.

The battlefield was just north of the village of Barnet. Warwick had placed his Lancastrian army astride the road, along the flat top of a ridge in the usual formation of three divisions, with a reserve in the rear. The best military man the earl had, his brother John Neville of Montagu, commanded the centre. Henry Holland, Duke of Exeter, who had also joined him, had charge of the left wing, and John de Vere, Earl of Oxford, the right. The Kingmaker himself was in the rear at the head of the reserve.

The King planned to post each of his three main divisions opposite the corresponding one of the enemy, but in the darkness they were placed a little too far to the right. Edward IV himself commanded the centre of the Yorkist army. With him was his unreliable brother George, Duke of Clarence. His other brother, Richard, Duke of Gloucester, headed the right wing, facing the Duke of Exeter's Lancastrian left. Lord Hastings had the left wing. A reserve was also held in the rear by the Yorkists.

Warwick had one other advantage besides greater numbers —a large battery of the cannon that were then coming into frequent use. All through the night they thundered, but Warwick thought the enemy camp was farther back than it actually was. So this tremendous bombardment came to nothing, for the balls screamed and whistled over Edward's Yorkist army and struck harmlessly in the rear.

By four o'clock on that Easter Sunday morning of April 14, 1471, both armies were astir. But at sunrise there was only a dim grayness, for a thick fog covered the battlefield. Nevertheless, the blast of Edward's trumpets signalled the start of the action.

Warwick's trumpets replied, and the battle was on. Both sides had posted archers on the left and right flanks of their armies. Between them were the long lines of men-at-arms with their pikes and other weapons. All, even the great lords, were dismounted in accordance with the usual custom of fighting afoot, using cavalry only to pursue a fleeing enemy.

The fog was typical of those which so often rolled in over the London area—so thick that in the city men called link boys waited on street corners with flaring torches to guide coaches and other vehicles through the streets. At Barnet it was impossible to see for more than ten yards, yet Warwick ordered his archers to fire as best they could. In the rear his cannon were still pounding away.

Richard, Duke of Gloucester, made the first move forward. He led his right wing up the slope of the ridge through the blinding mist. But since the Duke of Exeter's Lancastrian left wing was not directly ahead of them, Gloucester's men encountered nothing. Then Richard heard the clash of steel off to his left and knew the other two wings of each opposing army had met, but that he and his men must have passed the enemy's left wing. This was a piece of luck, for he could now swing his men around and outflank the Lancastrian left wing, attacking them from the side or rear. The enemy suddenly loomed out of the mist, and the two wings collided at close quarters.

The Duke of Exeter's Lancastrians, surprised at finding Richard of Gloucester's Yorkist wing attacking from that direction, fell back in confusion. But reinforcements came up to support them, their retreat was stopped and they held their ground. Now, for the first time, young Gloucester had a real chance to show his mettle in battle. He did not fail it, for he was in the very thick of the fight, swinging his battleaxe like a madman.

But this luck for Gloucester and his Yorkists was equally good for the Lancastrians at the other end of the battle line. The Earl of Oxford, groping ahead, discovered that he had outflanked the Yorkist left wing, where Hastings commanded. He had even better fortune, for by swinging his division and smashing it into Hastings' flank, he rolled it back and swept it into headlong retreat toward Barnet.

Many of the Earl of Oxford's elated Lancastrians pursued the fleeing Yorkists into Barnet. It was one of those mistakes that, for one reason or another, have often turned a victorious tide of battle into defeat. In Barnet the pursuing Lancastrians gave up the chase and fell to looting the town. It took the Earl of Oxford some time to reassemble them.

This done, he marched them back to the battlefield. He expected to strike Edward IV's centre from the rear and thus, with Lancastrian enemies coming at the King from both directions, destroy his force. Then came catastrophe.

When the Earl of Oxford's returning men came onto the battlefield, his ally, John Neville, Marquess of Montagu, in the centre, made them out dimly on his flank in the swirling fog. Oxford's banner was a star with streamers. Montagu's men mistook it for the Blazing Sun banner of Edward and thought they were being attacked by the Yorkist enemy. They sent a

storm of arrows whizzing into the ranks of Oxford's Lancastrians, their own fighting companions.

The arrows were not the worst of it. Because of them, some
of Oxford's Lancastrians thought John Neville of Montagu had
gone over to the King once more. It had happened often
enough before in this series of wars in which treachery was
rampant. Someone shouted: "Treason!" The cry spread
through both divisions. Some of Montagu's men, now recog-
nizing Oxford's Lancastrian troops, thought the cry meant that
Oxford was the traitor and had deserted to the Yorkists. Then
both Lancastrian divisions, each thinking the other had betrayed them, fled from the battlefield.

King Edward's great chance had come. The Duke of Gloucester's right wing, still battling gamely at the eastern end of
the ridge, was holding its own. The King called up his reserves
to join his centre and charged down the ridge.

Facing him now was Warwick, with his brother John Neville
of Montagu, his reserves and the remnant of those who had
not fled. The Kingmaker knew his situation was desperate.

"This is our last resource!" he shouted. "If we withstand this
charge the day is ours!"

Edward's Yorkists were now at the foot of the slope, a place
that became known as Dead Man's Bottom. There his centre
and Warwick's remaining men locked in a fierce, deadly, brief
struggle. John Neville, Marquess of Montagu, fell—some say
bravely in the fight; others say that some of the Lancastrians,
believing he was about to join the King, slew him.

Warwick learned of his brother's death and that the Earl of
Oxford had fled. His own battle line was beginning to crum-
ble. It was all over now.

The earl strode slowly and ponderously under the great

weight of his armour toward Wrotham Wood, to the north, where the horses had been tethered. If he could reach it he might ride to safety and to fight another day.

Too late. Floundering in the underbrush of Wrotham Wood, he was overtaken by Yorkists. With all the brutality of the Wars of the Roses, a slashing battleaxe felled him to the ground. Another foe pried open the visor of his helmet. Then came the swift thrust of a dagger.

Thus died Richard Neville, Earl of Warwick, under the banner of the Ragged Staff and Bear—the Kingmaker, beloved far and wide in England, a master diplomat and a brave and staunch if not brilliant general. And with him, it seemed, the House of Lancaster must perish too.

XI

Margaret of Anjou—
the Shattered Hope

With the battle of Barnet over, looting Yorkists stripped Richard Neville of Warwick's body bare, not only of armour but of the clothing beneath it. The next morning both his body and that of his brother John Neville of Montagu were piled in a rough cart and hauled to London. There, in St. Paul's Cathedral, covered only by loincloths, they lay on the pavement of the church for two days before burial, so that the people could see that the power of the House of Neville had been utterly destroyed.

As to the losses on both sides in the battle, the estimates are scanty and vary greatly, and what is known is only that probably between 1,000 and 3,000 in all were slain. It is said that more than 10,000 arrows were picked up on the field afterwards.

Henry VI, held under guard outside the battlefield, was taken back to London and the Tower. With him went the last of the Neville brothers, George, Archbishop of York, who had been restored as chamberlain during Warwick's brief and uncrowned reign.

In spite of his victory, Edward IV's recovered throne was still menaced. On the very day of the battle of Barnet, Margaret of Anjou, with her son Edward and his wife, the former Anne Neville, and Margaret's chief supporters in her exile had landed at Weymouth in Dorset on the Channel coast. They went on to nearby Cerne Abbey, where they were met a little later by Margaret's Lancastrian supporters in England. They included Edmund Beaufort, Duke of Somerset (who had succeeded to the title of his brother, Henry, who had turned Yorkist, but then became a traitor to Edward IV, only to lose his head after the battle of Hexham), and John Courtenay, Earl of Devon. These allies brought the news of Barnet, of Warwick's death and of how George, Duke of Clarence, and his army had proved false to the Lancastrians.

Margaret was shocked and disheartened. "All my hopes are lost!" she cried. "I must return to France!"

"Be not of faint heart, my lady Queen," the Duke of Somerset implored her. "All is not lost. The usurper Edward has been seriously weakened in the battle at Barnet. Your husband, good King Henry, though a prisoner in the Tower, is still alive. You have many friends who will flock to your aid, and if you strike now, before Edward has time to build new strength, you can win."

Margaret was not convinced. "I am thinking of my son, my only child!" she wailed. "If we remain in England I foresee only trouble and suffering, even death, for him."

"Jasper Tudor is in Wales with a force ready to come to your aid, my lady Queen," Somerset persisted. "He, with my help and that of the Earl of Devon, will reassemble the Lancastrian troops who escaped at Barnet. Devonshire, Cornwall and the west country have many others loyal to Lancaster."

Margaret of Anjou was wavering. "Could not my son Edward, the prince and rightful heir to the throne, be sent back to France in safety? For my own, I do not care."

"No," replied the Duke of Somerset, "it is most important that the people see both of you as you go forward to meet the usurper Edward."

And at last Margaret, though still fearful, agreed. The party moved west to Exeter in Devonshire, then north to Taunton and Wells in Somerset. As the Duke of Somerset had promised, loyal supporters streamed in all along the way to join her.

Margaret led the invading Lancastrian army, though the actual command was in the hands of the Duke of Somerset. Somerset appears to have been a leader of some ability, and the former Queen, seasoned by her previous campaigns, also had considerable military skill. By one or the other, or between them, it was decided to send small forces eastward to delude the King into thinking the whole Lancastrian army was marching on London. Actually it was going north through the west country. Eventually, Margaret intended to swing west into Wales and join Jasper Tudor with his force there.

The scheme seems to have worked. Two days after Margaret's landing, Edward IV heard of it and immediately began preparations to march. But for several days he did not know exactly where the Lancastrian army was or where it was really going.

The King, with his Yorkist army, marched out of London the short distance up the Thames to Windsor, where he waited until his scouts reported the whereabouts and movements of the enemy. Then he headed west with all speed.

The great danger to Margaret was that she might be cut off by the King's superior force before she could reach Wales. Between southern Wales and northern Devonshire and Somerset, the Bristol Channel cuts a long, wide slash in from the Atlantic. The Severn River, very wide at its mouth, flows southwestward into this channel and forms a part of the boundary between England and Wales. The first place where the Lancastrian army would be able to cross would be at the town of Gloucester, nearly forty miles above the Severn's mouth near Bristol. There the river was narrow and crossed by a bridge. It was for Gloucester that the Queen and her army were making with all possible speed.

It developed into a heartbreaking race in which this last, desperate effort by Margaret of Anjou was at stake. Her army was at Bath, near Bristol, on April 30, 1471, when the King's army arrived at Cirencester, some thirty miles to the northeast. Thus Edward was in an excellent position to cut the Lancastrians off by marching west to intercept them before they could reach Gloucester. The King was about fifteen miles nearer that town.

For some reason, possibly to pick up cannon and supplies, Margaret turned west from Bath a dozen miles to Bristol, rather than heading straight for Gloucester. This delay increased the risk to her even more. She decided her army must make a dash for Gloucester or she was lost.

At the same time she, the Duke of Somerset or both of them made a second smart military movement to deceive the King. They believed Edward would head for a little place called Sodbury, a few miles northeast of Bristol, in the lovely Cotswold Hills, to intercept the Lancastrian army. So the vanguard of Margaret's army was sent there.

The guess was exactly right. The King, believing the Lancastrians would be headed that way, marched for Sodbury.

When he arrived, the village was occupied by some of Margaret's men, while the rest of the Lancastrian vanguard had gone on.

For the second time, Edward had lost track of the enemy. While his men waited overnight, losing precious time, his scouts located the missing Lancastrian main army.

Margaret's force had marched twenty-two miles that day and reached the village of Berkeley in a state of exhaustion. But she had a lead over the King now of about twelve miles. She decided the soldiers must rest a few hours at least. They resumed their march at about one in the morning of May 3, 1471.

A Yorkist scout was watching. Two hours later he burst into the King's camp with the news. It was probably five before Edward's army could be roused, have breakfast and resume their pursuit. Their route took them over the Cotswolds and through the town of Cheltenham, a little east of Gloucester.

By midmorning the Lancastrians came in sight of Gloucester. There was no sign of the Yorkist army, and this cheered the tired men after their frantic march. The race was won!

Then came despair. To reach the bridge they would have to enter the town, but its gates were shut against them and its walls patrolled by armed men. The King had sent mounted couriers dashing ahead to warn Gloucester's governor, Sir Richard Beauchamp, a Yorkist, of the Lancastrians' approach.

Only one slim hope was left to Margaret and the Duke of Somerset. The next crossing was a ferry at Tewkesbury, about ten miles north. But ferrying the army across would be a slow operation. There was a bridge about six miles farther upstream. Somehow they had to plod on and reach it. The going would be slowed, as it already had been, by the army's heavy artillery.

The King was now hot on Margaret's heels. The weather was very warm for early May, and every step was agony for the footsore, weary Lancastrians. But Edward's situation was just as bad. He was on a parallel route a little to the east, rocky and hard going. There was no food to be found in that wild countryside, and his Yorkists passed only one small brook in which to slake their thirst.

About four that afternoon, Margaret's army reached Tewkesbury. Again it seemed that she might win the race, for once across the river they could destroy the bridge. But the men threw themselves to the ground, utterly spent. The army could go no farther. It halted and prepared to meet the King.

Luckily it was too late for Edward IV to catch up and give battle that day. The Queen's dog-tired Lancastrian army took up its position and camped on a low, flat ridge less than a mile south of Tewkesbury.

The King would have no easy time attacking this position. It was surrounded on every side by hills, valleys, deep ditches, hedges and brooks, and to the northwest by the Avon River, just before it emptied into the Severn beyond. As to the size of the two armies, Margaret's was probably larger, with about 5,000 men, while Edward had about 3,000 foot soldiers and an unknown number of mounted men.

The King's army camped about three miles to the south. Early the next morning, young Richard, Duke of Gloucester, in command of the vanguard, struggled across the forbidding countryside and took up a position facing the Lancastrian right wing. The King, commanding the centre and accompanied by his unreliable brother, George, Duke of Clarence, and Lord Hastings, at the head of the Yorkist right wing, followed.

Opposing Gloucester and commanding the Lancastrian right wing, as well as the army itself, was the Duke of Somerset. At the head of the Lancastrian left wing, opposite Hastings, was the Earl of Devon. The honour of commanding the Lancastrian centre had been given to Margaret's precious son, Prince Edward, then only seventeen. But the actual leadership was in the hands of John, Lord Wenlock—a risky choice indeed, for he had already twice proved himself a traitor. At the second battle of St. Albans he had fought for the Lancastrians. Then he had gone over to the Yorkists at Towton. Now he was back with the Lancastrians—for how long, who knew? In the gap between the three Lancastrian divisions were Margaret's cannon.

As had happened at Barnet, the bold Richard of Gloucester made the first move, against the Duke of Somerset, but the going was so bad that it was impossible to get at him. The only result was a hail of arrows from both sides and some cannon fire.

The Duke of Somerset saw his chance for a clever piece of military strategy. Since the Duke of Gloucester had been unable to reach him, he led his Lancastrian division westward under the cover of the many hedges and underbrush, outflanked the Yorkist left wing and charged in on Richard of Gloucester's flank. But he failed to shake young Richard's coolness; the Yorkists fell back a short distance, but held their ground.

King Edward had already anticipated such a move by the Duke of Somerset. Just to the west of the battle lines was a small, wooded knoll. There, well concealed, he had posted about two hundred spearmen. Once Somerset had passed them, they charged in on his rear, raising such a tremendous shout that it seemed there must be many more of them. At the same time, Richard of Gloucester led his men ahead in a furious charge.

Somerset's Lancastrian division, beset from front and rear,

fell to pieces. His men fled, helter-skelter, making for the Avon River to the northwest. Stumbling through ditches, they reached an open meadow between the battlefield and the river, where the Yorkists overtook them, killing so many that the place gained the name of Bloody Meadow.

While the Duke of Somerset's Lancastrians were trying to flee from the murderous trap they had fallen into, Lord Wenlock, in the Lancastrian centre, did nothing to help the duke. Somerset, who was mounted and had not joined his division's retreat, rode up to Wenlock.

"Traitor!" he screamed in a fury. "If you had come to my aid we could have routed them! You betrayed me!" And with one mighty sweep of his battleaxe, he clove Wenlock's skull in two.

The Yorkists had the edge now, and their skilled commander, the King, took instant advantage of it. He led his centre division in a charge, smashing straight into the now leaderless Lancastrian centre. Richard, Duke of Gloucester, with his opposite enemy defeated, swung in to aid Edward and outflank the Lancastrian centre. It too fell to pieces and fled toward the Avon. Pursuing Yorkists cut down many, and others drowned trying to cross the river.

Margaret's son, young Prince Edward, seems to have been utterly helpless after Wenlock was killed. He spurred his horse in a desperate attempt to reach Tewkesbury. A detachment commanded by the Duke of Clarence overhauled him. One swift sword slash put an end to the prince's life and Margaret's last hope.

What was left of the Lancastrian army, the Earl of Devon's left wing, then crumbled and was swept into retreat. The King had won a complete and overwhelming victory. Over a thousand men are said to have been killed in the battle.

The Duke of Somerset and about a dozen other Lancastrian leaders, along with some of the soldiers, managed to gain the shelter of Tewkesbury Abbey in the hope of obtaining sanctuary there. The King galloped up to the abbey, dismounted and pounded furiously on its door with his sword. It was opened by the abbot.

"I pray you, your Grace, do not defile a holy place!" the clergyman pleaded.

It melted the King's rage. "I will grant a pardon to all who have sought refuge with you, good abbot," he said. Then he asked, "Who is within?" And as far as Edmund Beaufort, Duke of Somerset, and his companions were concerned, Edward forgot his promise when he learned they were among the refugees, especially since Tewkesbury Abbey was not a duly appointed place of sanctuary.

The Duke of Somerset, the Earl of Devon and the other lords were seized and tried before Richard, Duke of Gloucester, as Constable of England, and the Duke of Norfolk, Marshal of England, a kind of master sheriff. They were promptly condemned and beheaded in the Tewkesbury marketplace.

One last enemy remained to be rounded up. A searching party found Margaret in a religious house, where she had retired before the battle. The searchers saw a woman crushed and broken by the news of Prince Edward's death and the defeat. There was nothing left of the bold and dauntless Queen who had fought so long, so tirelessly and so hopelessly for her husband and son.

"I place myself at the King's command," she told the party.

On May 21, 1471, King Edward IV entered London in the greatest triumphal procession of his reign. His Yorkist army marched proudly to the blasts of trumpets and clarions under the battle banners with their emblems and bright colours. The

King had given his valiant youngest brother, Richard, Duke of Gloucester, the honour of leading it. Behind him came Lord Hastings, then the King. Bringing up the rear of the army rode the other royal brother, George, Duke of Clarence. Last of all, slumped with unseeing eyes on a litter, came Margaret of Anjou. The watching crowd threw stones and mud and reviled her.

The King had one more objective to be carried out. Most historians are agreed that it was set in motion at a council with his advisers that evening. When it was ended, the story goes, Edward IV wrote out an order addressed to Lord John Dudley, Constable of the Tower of London, and handed it to Richard of Gloucester.

"Bear this to Dudley, my brother," he commanded, appointing a delegation of other lords to accompany Gloucester.

The next morning Henry VI was found dead in his cell in the Tower. Some reports have it that Richard, Duke of Gloucester, himself did the deed, but no one really knows. What is quite certain is that the Lancastrian King was murdered by Edward IV's order. That night Henry's body was borne to St. Paul's, where it lay on a bier with only the face exposed, until it was borne up the Thames and buried in the chapel of Chertsey Abbey.

As for Henry's wretched widow, she was kept in the Tower for a time, then in various other places, including several castles, with an ample income and servants to attend her. Edward IV finally extorted a ransom of £50,000 for her from Louis XI and she was allowed to return to France.

One cannot help feeling deep pity for this indomitable woman who had lost everything she cherished and hoped for. True, Shakespeare called her "stern, obdurate, flinty, rough, remorseless" and the "she wolf of France," having a "tiger's heart wrapped in a woman's hide." True, although she is said to have been very beautiful when she was young, the effigy that rests on top of her tomb in Westminster Abbey is that of a hard-faced, hook-nosed woman. Yet she is to be admired for her unshakable determination and her loyalty to and protection of her weak husband.

And now Edward IV was indeed unchallenged King of England.

XII

The King Is Dead!
Long Live the King!

Edward IV reigned over England for twelve more years. He was a good king as rulers went in those days. His reign was beset by a good many troubles, but on the whole it was peaceful. And Edward brought such prosperity to England as it had never seen before.

The King had his faults. He could be cruel and merciless, but that was a way of life for monarchs in the fifteenth century. He was unfaithful to his Queen, the former Elizabeth Woodville, who bore him two sons and seven daughters, though two of the girls died young. He loved pleasure too much, ate enormous quantities of food and drank too much. Richard Neville, Earl of Warwick, is once said to have remarked, "I would rather fight fifty battles *for* him than sup once *with* him."

There were still some threats to Edward's throne. At the very time of the battle of Tewkesbury, one of Warwick's supporters landed in Kent from Calais, gathered a force of loyal friends to the Ragged Staff and reached London Bridge before they were thrown back by a force of Edward's men who had been left to guard the capital.

There was also Jasper Tudor, who had tried desperately but failed to join Margaret of Anjou before the Tewkesbury battle. Jasper and his nephew, Henry Tudor, were forced to flee into exile in Brittany. But the two Welshmen were still hopeful.

Edward promptly reorganized the government, with his chief supporters taking over the high offices. Then he set himself to improving England's prosperity and the people's welfare. He knew how sick they were of war, its privations and the heavy taxes they had been forced to bear. With great wisdom he imposed no new taxes and, in spite of his love of luxury, resolved to live within his income.

Indeed, that was not difficult. Edward IV's wealth had been increased enormously by the estates of the Lancastrian nobles which he had confiscated after they had been slain or executed or had fled to exile. Also, a number of wealthy religious establishments had voluntarily given him gifts of cash. In addition, the King became a trader, through agents who handled these business affairs, sharing in England's booming export and import trade.

There were troubles, nevertheless. One of the most annoying concerned Edward's brother George, Duke of Clarence, always a troublemaker, and his quarrel with his brother, Richard, Duke of Gloucester, over Warwick's daughter Anne. When her husband, Prince Edward, was slain at Tewkesbury, she had been with Margaret when the former Queen was captured after the battle.

Anne had been sent to Coventry and placed in charge of the Duke of Clarence's wife, Isabel, her sister. No doubt Richard of Gloucester saw her there, since they had been childhood friends when he had been under Warwick's charge at Middle-ham. At any rate, Richard of Gloucester obtained the King's permission to marry Anne.

But Richard's older brother, the Duke of Clarence, had no intention of allowing this. Warwick's widow, the Countess of Warwick, also had large estates of her own, which Clarence had seized in the name of his wife, the countess' daughter. Since Anne was also the countess' daughter, she was heiress to half the countess' property. Clarence wanted it all, and was determined to have it by preventing Anne's marriage to Richard.

So when Richard appeared at Clarence's London house to claim his bride, Clarence confronted him.

"I have come for Anne, since our brother the King has graciously granted me permission to wed her," the Duke of Gloucester explained.

"She is not in my household," Clarence declared tersely.

Richard glowered at him. "Of course she is here. Do you dare disobey the King?"

"You are welcome to satisfy yourself that she is not here," his brother sneered.

"Where is she, then?"

George, Duke of Clarence, shrugged. "I know not nor care not. I have no wardship over the lady, and I am not respon-sible for her whereabouts."

"I will find her," said Richard of Gloucester grimly. And he did, where his brother had hidden her in the house of a friend, disguised as a maid. Gloucester placed her in sanctuary at the church of St. Martin-le-Grand. Then he sought his brother Edward's aid in settling the dispute. The King called his brothers to a council.

It was a long and stormy session. The King was in a quandary. He had great affection for Richard and was grateful for his steadfast loyalty, which had never wavered. That was far from true in the Duke of Clarence's case, but he was dangerous. Edward wanted no more trouble with his brother George; somehow the quarrel would have to be settled to satisfy both dukes.

At last a compromise was reached. In return for the Duke of Clarence's agreement that his brother might marry Anne Neville, Richard of Gloucester gave his older brother all of Warwick's property which the King had granted him, except for Middleham and some of the other estates in Yorkshire. Also, he let Clarence have the high office of Great Chamberlain of England, which Edward had given Richard of Gloucester. Clarence was also to be given the earldoms of Warwick and Salisbury.

Since Richard, Duke of Gloucester, and Anne Neville were related through his mother, who had been born Cecily Neville, a marriage between them required a special dispensation from the Church. But Richard had no time or patience to wait for such formalities. He took Anne out of sanctuary and married her immediately.

In spite of his grudging agreement, George, Duke of Clarence, was still resentful. He brooded, and since intrigue and troublemaking were his way of life, he began plotting again. This time it was with the Earl of Oxford, the Lancastrian who had fled to refuge in France after the battle of Barnet, and with King Louis XI of France and George Neville, Archbishop of York.

Edward IV had always had a great affection for George Neville as well as George's brother Warwick. He had imprisoned George in the Tower after Tewkesbury, but he soon let him out and pardoned him. The archbishop, a born schemer, repaid the King by joining the Duke of Clarence's plot.

The Earl of Oxford, cruising off the English coast with a fleet, had been seizing English merchant ships. In the late summer of 1473 he took St. Michael's mount, a rocky island off the tip of Cornwall, and tried to raise a rebel army of Cornishmen, at the same time seeking Louis XI's aid. Neither responded, and Oxford was forced to surrender in return for his life.

Edward suspected that George Neville had been in the conspiracy. He decided to repay the archbishop in Neville's own deceitful coin. He sent word he was coming to George's Hertfordshire manor, "The Moor," supposedly to go hunting with Neville. The archbishop was elated at this apparent return to the King's favour. He had hidden his silver and other valuables after Tewkesbury lest they be seized. Now he brought them out, prepared a lavish feast with the best wines and waited for his royal guest's arrival.

To his consternation, only a royal messenger arrived, with a summons for Neville to come immediately to Windsor. There, trembling with fear, he was seized and imprisoned for a night in the Tower, then in a remote fortress and finally in another castle, close to Calais. He was unhappy in France, and the King finally relented and let him return to England, where he soon died, in 1476. And this was the end of the last Neville who could possibly cause Edward IV trouble.

England was happy to be at peace, but the King, a warrior by nature, was not. He yearned to restore to England some of the rich French provinces that had been lost before the Wars of the Roses began. He made up his mind to invade France.

It was some time before he could carry out his plan. The trouble was that it would cost a great deal of money. So he convened Parliament and told the members of his design to recover such rich French provinces as Normandy, Gascony and Guienne. If they would grant him the money to pay, feed and equip at least 13,000 archers for a year, he would do the rest. Parliament appropriated the money.

It was soon spent, however, and proved not to be enough. So the King revived the ancient custom of benevolences. Wealthy lords, knights, clergymen and merchants were "invited" to make gifts of money to the King. In doing so, Edward was almost as bad as the many highwaymen roaming the roads of England, for those asked for benevolences had no choice but to give. Some did so willingly; others gave most unwillingly, but fearing the King's disfavour they paid, hoping to reap rewards later on. And thus the extra money was raised.

Edward had made an alliance against France with Duke Charles of Burgundy, the husband of his sister, the Duchess Margaret. He wanted the duke's aid to strengthen his own army of some 11,000 archers, 1,500 men-at-arms and much artillery that crossed the Channel to Calais in June, 1475. Unfortunately Charles, who was called "the Rash," was a most unreliable man. It was mid-July before he arrived at Calais—without his army, which was off besieging a small city in Germany.

Nevertheless, the duke was bursting with enthusiasm. "You have a host which can sweep through all of France, your Grace!" he exclaimed. "Join me, and we will start by pillaging Lorraine."

King Edward stared at him. Lorraine was far to the east. Why not Normandy or some other, nearer province? This was indeed a crazy idea. He politely ignored the suggestion, and

Duke Charles galloped away. Then the King, in council with Richard, Duke of Gloucester, the Duke of Clarence and other leaders, decided to move southeastward to the Burgundian city of St. Quentin, from which they might strike into France. But although Duke Charles joined them during their march, the gates of St. Quentin were shut against them by its Burgundian governor.

With that, all King Edward's faith in the duke vanished, for he suspected this was some sort of treachery. But he soon had a more serious problem to face. Word came that Louis XI of France, with a powerful army, was at Compiègne, only about forty miles away.

Edward believed he could beat the French, but his money was almost gone, and the countryside ahead of them had been laid waste of all food by Louis. He decided to try diplomacy to see if Louis might be willing to make peace on terms favourable to the English. He let word that he might negotiate leak through to the French King.

Louis jumped at the offer, for he was afraid of the military genius of the great English warrior. He suggested that envoys from both sides meet halfway between the two armies. Of all the English leaders, only Richard, Duke of Gloucester, stood firmly against the plan. Perhaps he felt it was like the old nursery rhyme:

> *The King of France went up the hill,*
> *With forty thousand men;*
> *The King of France came down the hill,*
> *And ne'er went up again.*

Only now it would be the King of England who marched against the French King and back again. What would the

English people think of it—those who had given benevolences, and poorer ones who were being taxed for this war to restore England's lost French domains?

But once Edward IV made up his mind, it was made up. And indeed it proved a wise choice. Louis XI was so frightened that he immediately accepted the terms offered by the English. He would pay King Edward 75,000 gold crowns at once, and 50,000 crowns a year after that, marry his son, the Dauphin or Crown Prince, to Edward's eldest daughter Elizabeth and make a private alliance in which each side agreed to assist the other if rebellions arose in either country.

Louis was so delighted with a settlement that enabled him to keep the precious disputed French provinces that he threw the nearby town of Amiens open to the English army. He had long tables set up outside the gates, fairly groaning with venison pasties, other meats and delicacies and plenty of good strong wine. Inside the town, nine inns were reserved for the soldiers at the French King's expense, with more food and drink. After they had gorged themselves on all this free hospitality for three days, most of them were roaring drunk, lying like so many befuddled pigs in the streets. Edward became alarmed lest the French take advantage of this, and he finally managed to get them back to their camp.

Then, on August 20, 1475, the two monarchs met in the middle of a bridge over the River Somme at Picquigny. They made a strange contrast as they advanced to greet each other. Edward IV, with his towering stature and powerful, oxlike frame, was a picture of royal magnificence. He wore a gown of cloth of gold lined with red satin, and a black velvet cap studded with a glittering, jewelled fleur-de-lis. He dwarfed Louis XI, who looked like anything but a king in his usual dress of drab, cheap cloth.

Each king bowed low to the other. Then, each with one hand on a piece of the True Cross, they signed the treaty. For some minutes afterwards they chatted as amiably as if they had been lifelong friends rather than, often enough, deadly enemies.

Richard of Gloucester had been right enough in his fears that the English people would not like what had happened. They were dismayed when Edward IV, whom they considered the greatest fighting man in the world, returned without an arrow having been sprung from its bow or a cannon fired—and with none of England's lost territory recovered. Yet in the long run Edward proved to have been right.

Certainly London did not fail to appreciate what the King had accomplished. To the great merchants the peace meant more trade and thus riches; to the artisans and other working people, more work and wages. The Londoners gave the King a tumultuous welcome home. As for those in the English countryside, they soon forgot their dismay. They were all tired of war and its burdens. And under Edward's rule England became a better place to live. He was never the popular figure Richard, Earl of Warwick, had been, but he earned the people's respect.

Of course, the King still had problems. One of the first to be solved was that of his brother George, Duke of Clarence. The duke was soon making trouble again.

His chance came when Charles the Rash, Duke of Burgundy, died on January 5, 1477, fighting as usual, in a siege of Nancy in Lorraine. The Duke of Clarence's wife, Isabel, Warwick's elder daughter, had died the year before. Why not marry Mary, the daughter of Charles the Rash and his own sister Margaret, now Dowager Duchess of Burgundy? What difference did it make that Mary was Clarence's own niece? It would mean that he would become Duke of Burgundy, with all the power that went with the title.

Strangely enough, Mary's mother seems to have favoured wedding her daughter to her favourite brother George, Duke of Clarence. But the marriage never took place. For one thing, Mary would have none of it. More important, King Edward IV said NO in a way that left no doubt he meant it. He had never trusted his brother, and as Duke of Burgundy, Clarence could make trouble for England, perhaps even invade it and try to seize the crown he so bitterly resented his brother for wearing.

"Whom the Gods would destroy, they first make mad," wrote the poet Longfellow. It applies well to George, Duke of Clarence. First he flew into a fury; then he sulked and made himself as obnoxious as possible to everyone. When he did appear at Court he refused to eat or drink, making it plain to all that he expected to be poisoned.

Then he did what would make it seem that the gods had indeed made him mad. In Somersetshire, on April 12, 1477, an armed force he had sent burst into the house of Ankarette Twynylo, who had been one of his dead wife's trusted and intimate servants. They whisked her off to the town of Warwick, where she was charged with poisoning Clarence's wife. The duke had bribed judges and jury, and Ankarette was speedily condemned and hanged.

What Clarence had done was very close to treason, for he had taken the administration of justice into his hands in a case that was the King's sole responsibility. Edward IV was now fully aware that Clarence intended to make himself King if he could.

Yet the duke rushed on to his doom. He began spreading scandalous rumours about his brother : Edward IV practiced the Black Art—witchcraft—and had used it to poison some of his subjects; the King meant to destroy him "as a candle consumeth in burning"; his brother was not a legitimate son of his father, the slain Richard, Duke of York (and therefore he, Clarence, was the rightful heir to the throne); and Edward's marriage to Elizabeth Woodville had not been legal.

Early in June, 1477, the last thread of the King's patience snapped. Louis XI, pretending a friendship which had never really existed and simply trying to stir up trouble, informed Edward IV that his spies had learned that the Duke of Clarence's true reason for seeking to marry the dead Duke of Burgundy's daughter was to enable him to seize the crown of England.

The enraged King summoned his brother to Westminster. In the presence of the Lord Mayor of London, he accused Clarence of trying to overthrow the laws of the kingdom by taking justice into his own hands. Then he summoned guards and sent Clarence to the Tower, a prisoner.

For all the Duke of Clarence's spitefulness, Richard, Duke of Gloucester, pleaded with the King to spare their brother's life. But Edward stood firm, probably because of the Woodvilles, since they had not forgotten Clarence's part in the slaying of the elder Earl Rivers and his son John during Warwick's invasion.

The Duke of Clarence lay in the Tower all the rest of 1477. He was still there on January 16, 1478, when the King's second son, Richard, Duke of York, was married to Anne Mowbray, heiress of the Duke of Norfolk. It seems unbelievable, but the little prince was only four years old, and his bride six! But there was always a reason for such royal and noble marriages, common in the fifteenth century—not love, of course, but power, money and politics.

As though the King had been waiting to get this festive business out of the way, he had summoned Parliament to meet on the very next day, January 17. A bill of attainder was brought against the Duke of Clarence for high treason, with the King as the only witness against him. The bill was passed, and Clarence was condemned to death.

Suddenly the King hesitated. Cruel though he could be, he could not bring himself to order his brother's execution. But the Woodvilles were using all their influence upon him, and a month later Parliament itself urged Edward to act.

That night George, Duke of Clarence, died in the Tower. Just how it was done, by whom or by whose order, is an unsolved mystery of English history. A story, almost certainly false, went about London that the duke was drowned in one of the huge casks called butts, filled with his favourite drink, Malmsey wine.

Five years of life remained to Edward IV, and he made good use of them for England's welfare, governing justly though firmly. Justice needed tightening in the kingdom, for the roads still teemed with bands of highwaymen, who set upon travellers, robbing and often killing them. Even the many people who made pilgrimages to holy shrines bearing gifts were forced to hand them over. So the King made journeys throughout the kingdom, visiting the courts to see that the laws against crime were strictly enforced. The result was not only harsher sentences for criminals but stiffer fines for other lawbreakers. This benefited the King, for by custom the money went to line the royal purse. What with this and the money he made in trading, Edward IV became one of England's wealthiest men.

Trade boomed, for he made commercial treaties with the Low Countries which increased exports and imports. And for the most part there was peace. In 1480, Scottish raids across the border began to cause trouble, but in 1482 Edward sent Richard, Duke of Gloucester, north with an army. It not only defeated the Scots but recovered prized Berwick, which Margaret of Anjou had given them in return for their aid.

As for the King's sons, the younger, Richard, was kept at Westminster, but Edward, Prince of Wales, had been sent to Ludlow Castle in the west country when he was three years old. His mother had seen to that. Although the young prince was under the care of John Alcock, Bishop of Rochester, the governor of the castle was Anthony Woodville, the new Earl Rivers, elder son of the executed Richard Woodville.

Thus, all through his younger days, Prince Edward was surrounded by Woodvilles. But he did receive excellent though rigorous training for a king-to-be. His mornings were spent in study, the afternoons in learning the arts of knighthood and military training that all young men of royal or noble blood must know. But he saw little of his father or mother.

At his palace in Westminster the King, though he had no Warwick to handle the affairs of state, found an able substitute in Richard, Duke of Gloucester. Thus Edward IV was free to enjoy the pleasures of eating, drinking and dallying with lovely ladies. He grew enormously fat and sluggish, no longer the powerful, muscular warrior he had once been.

However, he did not devote all his time to these pleasures. He was interested in literature and spent much time in collecting and adding to his library the richly illuminated books done so laboriously before printing came into use. William Caxton, an Englishman who had learned the art of printing in the Low Countries, had returned to his native island and set up a printing establishment in London. The King was intensely interested, and visited Caxton in his shop.

Edward IV had a great admiration for learning. He had studied Greek, and he gave gifts and grants to several colleges. And certainly his greatest contribution to art, and the best remembered, was his reconstruction of St. George's Chapel at Windsor Castle. This gem of beauty and architecture is now visited by thousands of tourists each year.

The King had only one small threat to his throne to worry him—Henry Tudor. True, there was a question as to the legality of Henry's claim to it as a descendant of King Edward III. Nevertheless, Edward IV itched to get his hands on Henry Tudor.

Henry and his uncle, Jasper Tudor, the deposed Earl of Pembroke, were still living in exile in Brittany. As the story is told by Polydore Vergil, a historian of the period, King Edward IV offered Duke Francis of Brittany a rich ransom for Henry Tudor. Duke Francis seems to have been willing, and surrendered Henry to envoys Edward IV sent there. But then the duke, apparently afraid Louis XI would object, changed his mind. A rescue party seized Henry Tudor just as he was about to be put aboard a ship for England. Duke Francis then placed him in sanctuary. However, he did promise Edward that both Henry and Jasper Tudor would be carefully watched, and he kept his word to the end of Edward IV's reign.

In 1483, Edward IV was in his forty-second year. In general, people died earlier in the fifteenth century than today, but no one, least of all Edward himself, had any idea that this hearty man in the very prime of life could be near his end. But his days as King had been ones of high living. Dissipation had taken its toll.

In the latter part of March, 1483, Edward was at his favourite castle of Windsor. On March 30 he was suddenly taken ill. Soon he could no longer sit up and was forced to lie on his right side. And on April 30, 1483, Edward IV died. He was buried in great pomp at Windsor, in St. George's Chapel, where his body rests today.

Proclamations of royal deaths contain the phrase: "The King is dead! Long live the King [meaning the new one]!" Edward IV's elder son, thirteen years old, was now King Edward V. Under Edward IV's will, the boy King was placed under the care of Richard, Duke of Gloucester, as Protector.

XIII

The Little Princes

At Middleham Castle a mounted courier charged across the drawbridge bearing the news of Edward IV's death and a message to Richard, Duke of Gloucester, from Lord Hastings: "The King has left all to your protection—goods, heir, realm. Secure the person of our sovereign, Lord Edward V, and get you to London."

Young Edward V was in the possession of Anthony Woodville, Earl Rivers, at Ludlow. If the Woodvilles decided to disobey the dead King's will and keep Richard, Duke of Gloucester, from becoming Protector, there would be trouble. Richard's anxiety over this increased when a second message from Lord Hastings arrived, saying that the Woodvilles had taken over all affairs in the capital.

Should he assemble as strong a force as possible to enter London and assert his rights as Protector? Evidently Henry Stafford, Duke of Buckingham, after Richard the second highest-ranking nobleman in England, thought so. He sent Richard word from South Wales that he was prepared to join Gloucester's cavalcade with a thousand men if they were needed. But Duke Richard decided on caution. He wrote the Duke of Buckingham that he was planning to join Earl Rivers and the boy King on their progress to London and would be glad to have the duke meet him on the road, but he asked that Buckingham have only a small escort, not more than three hundred men. Gloucester himself decided to march with the same number.

Duke Richard's cavalcade moved south from Yorkshire toward Nottingham. On the way a courteous message from Anthony Woodville, Earl Rivers, arrived, suggesting that Gloucester meet him at Northampton on April 29. But when Richard reached Nottingham on April 26 alarming news came from Lord Hastings. The Woodvilles were making preparations to crown Edward V at once and take the protectorship away from Duke Richard.

Gloucester knew that all this might cause war between his own supporters, who hated the Woodvilles, and those of Anthony Woodville, Earl Rivers, and the now Dowager Queen Elizabeth, Edward IV's widow. Nevertheless, he was confident that he could win.

Meanwhile, at Westminster, the dead King's widow and her eldest son by her first marriage, the Marquess of Dorset, were frantically trying to eliminate Gloucester as Protector. The marquess was not a strong person, but he was under his mother's domineering control. Before Edward IV's council he declared that the new King, Edward V, should be crowned as soon as possible, and suggested May 4 as the date.

The council wavered. A number of its members were alarmed at the Woodvilles' moves in defiance of Edward IV's will. Nevertheless, the Woodvilles went right ahead. A letter was sent to the family's leader, Anthony, Earl Rivers, saying that he and the young King must reach London by May 1. They hoped he might beat Richard of Gloucester, who would thus find Edward V crowned and his own protectorship gone when he arrived in the capital.

On April 20 Gloucester reached Northampton. There was no sign of Earl Rivers and the new King. He learned that their army of 2,000 men had passed through the town and continued southward. Gloucester decided to spend the night in the town.

Soon afterward, visitors arrived at Richard's inn—Earl Rivers and his attendants.

"I have come, my lord Protector, at the command of his Grace, the King, to convey his greetings to his beloved uncle," the earl, Anthony Woodville, announced.

The use of Gloucester's new title, if Earl Rivers really meant it, was encouraging. Richard greeted him with equal politeness and then asked, "Where is his Grace, the King, my beloved nephew?"

"He has gone to Stony Stratford to pass the night," Woodville replied. "We feared that Northampton could not offer accommodations suitable to our new sovereign."

Stony Stratford was fourteen miles closer to London. Was this, Gloucester wondered, the real reason for the King's remaining there? Nevertheless, he offered Earl Rivers all hospitality. While they were chatting amiably over supper, the Duke of Buckingham arrived. The three lingered late over wine, talking in the friendliest way. Then Earl Rivers left for quarters he had taken at another inn.

The two dukes, Gloucester and Buckingham, did not retire, however. They met in a long discussion of what they should do. At last they decided on a plan.

At dawn the next morning, Earl Rivers' inn was surrounded

by armed men, with guards posted on the road to Stony Stratford, permitting no one to pass. The two dukes then went to
Rivers' inn, where he greeted them as cordially as though
nothing had happened.

"I do not understand this," he said. "Pray, what is amiss?"

"You are under arrest," said Richard of Gloucester.

The Dukes of Buckingham and Gloucester then mounted
and spurred their horses in a dash for Stony Stratford. When
they reached the town they found young King Edward V with
his escort of armed men mounted to ride to London. The
dukes dismounted, advanced and fell to their knees before the
new King, greeting him with humble respect. Then Richard
of Gloucester said "Your Grace, I have serious matters to discuss with you."

The King, with some of his party and the Dukes of Gloucester and Buckingham, then went into his lodgings.

"My purpose in coming here, your Grace, is to warn you of
evil," the Duke of Gloucester began. "Certain ones of your late
father's ministers encouraged him to excesses which ruined
his health. They must be removed from power so that they
may not act in such treasonable fashion toward yourself."

"I protest—" one of Edward V's party began

"Be silent!" Buckingham ordered him.

"These men about you seek your life," Gloucester went on,
speaking to Edward V. "For your safety, your Grace, I have
placed Anthony Woodville, Earl Rivers, under arrest at
Northampton."

"But these are my friends, uncle!" the boy cried. "Although I
am young, I am certain that my nobles and my mother will
assist me in governing the kingdom."

"It is for men to reign over England, not women," the Duke

of Buckingham said. "Your mother has no authority to rule. You have been deceived, your Grace."

Richard of Gloucester then spoke: "I served your father in council and in battle for many years, your Grace. King Edward IV appointed me Protector of the kingdom and of you because of my experience and my reputation, and because I am your uncle. Is your Grace content to abide by your father's wish?"

Edward V yielded, though his voice shook a little as he replied, "I will be content with the government my father arranged for me."

"Your Grace, we must go to Northampton until I receive word that it is safe for you to proceed to London," said Gloucester. And with that he placed two of the young king's party under arrest and told the armed royal escort that it must disperse and go home quietly. Although their numbers were greater, the men obeyed.

The news of Richard of Gloucester's success threw the Woodvilles at Westminster into a panic. Suddenly the lords who had fawned on them and done their bidding had no interest in fighting Duke Richard. Dowager Queen Elizabeth, with nine-year-old Prince Richard, her daughters and others of her family, fled to the sanctuary of Westminster Abbey.

Lord Hastings, Edward IV's dearest friend and the most popular nobleman in the kingdom, was jubilant, especially when Richard, Duke of Gloucester, wrote saying that he had not captured the young King but only saved him and the kingdom. This enabled Hastings to convince the royal council that Gloucester should be received in London as Protector.

And so it was settled. Having sent his prisoners to the safety of castles in faraway Yorkshire, Gloucester rode for London with the new King. On May 4 the cavalcade entered the

capital with the usual pomp and magnificence—cheering popu-
lace, all the many bells of London pealing in tones from bass
to soprano, the London authorities brilliant in fur-trimmed
scarlet, the burgesses or leading citizens in purple. Young
Edward V wore blue velvet, and on his right rode Richard,
Duke of Gloucester, and on his left the Duke of Buckingham,
both dressed in black as mourning for Edward IV. The procession wound its way through the City to Edward V's tem-
porary lodgings in the Bishop of London's palace.

The coronation was postponed. Gloucester took up his
duties as Protector, replacing all the Woodville government
officials with followers of his own. Edward V was King in
name; Richard, Duke of Gloucester, in reality.

Proper lodgings would have to be found for the King. The
Duke of Buckingham suggested the Tower—not as a prison,
of course, for it was also a palace—and in May the new King
was installed there in apartments of state. And now that Gloucester had full control as Protector, Edward V could be
crowned. June 2 was set for the great event.

Meanwhile, the Duke of Buckingham rose to greater power
than ever before. Gloucester conferred high office after high
office upon him. Buckingham was becoming to Richard what
Warwick had once been to Edward IV—friend, ally and right-
hand man.

Although Lord Hastings kept all the high posts he had
enjoyed as Edward IV's closest friend, he was unhappy and
jealous over Buckingham's rise. He and several other councillors who were also dissatisfied for one reason or another, including Lord Stanley, took to holding private meetings at
each other's houses.

A whisper of these meetings reached Richard of Gloucester.

He set agents to watching Hastings and the others. Buckingham too had a part in this spying. The Protector was suspicious. For one thing, he knew that Lord Stanley was not trustworthy; he had shifted from one side to the other in the past. So had two others of the group—John Morton, Bishop of Ely, and Thomas Rotherham, who had succeeded John Neville as Archbishop of York.

Buckingham learned that Hastings and his friends were ready to join the Woodvilles, who wanted nothing so much as to be rid of Duke Richard as Protector. Gloucester immediately sent an appeal to the north for an army to fight the Woodvilles, and asked the Earl of Northumberland to lead it.

Meanwhile, the Protector struck a swift, deadly blow at the conspirators. He summoned Hastings, Stanley and Bishops Morton and Rotherham, along with Buckingham and other loyal advisers, to a conference in the White Tower, the main fortress of the Tower of London. They met on Friday the 13th, a sinister date in modern superstition.

All were assembled around a table there when Richard, Duke of Gloucester, entered, his countenance as black as an August thunderhead. He threw himself into his chair and demanded, "What shall be done with those that compass and imagine the destruction of me, being so near of blood to the King, and Protector of the Realm?"

Lord Hastings, who had not the slightest idea that Gloucester knew of his treachery, replied, "They are worthy to suffer the worst."

He was pronouncing his own death sentence. Gloucester glowered at the plotters, then hurled a charge at them: "You are all guilty of plotting with the Woodvilles against my protectorship!"

Hastings' face was ashen. "I deny it, my Lord!" he cried.

"Treason!" shouted Richard of Gloucester. "Treason, I say!"

"It is a lie!" Hastings shot back vehemently.

Gloucester brought his fist crashing down on the table. At this signal a band of armed men burst into the room. There was a fierce struggle, with the conspirators trying to defend themselves and flee, but they were seized and rendered helpless.

Gloucester wasted no time on Hastings, who was dragged from the White Tower to the green outside, his head laid on a piece of wood and chopped off. One may stand on that green today, the same place where, half a century later, King Henry VIII's wife, Anne Boleyn, was beheaded. It is a pleasant, grassy lawn where the famous ravens of the Tower mince about, with nothing save a small paved area marking the execution spot to remind the visitor of its bloody past.

Bishops Morton and Rotherham were imprisoned in the Tower. Lord Stanley alone was allowed to go to his own lodgings, though under guard there. He was later set free, and so were the bishops.

Richard, Duke of Gloucester, now more secure as Protector, assembled the royal council and told them what he had discovered about the conspiracy. His evidence convinced them that he had acted to prevent treason.

"Now," Gloucester continued, "I would discuss the matter of the Dowager Queen Elizabeth and her younger son Richard, Duke of York. She must be induced to come forth with the boy prince. Our new King needs the companionship of his brother. And what will the people think if the King is crowned without young Richard present? I say to you, the Dowager Queen is holding him as a hostage so that she may regain control of the government and turn me out of my rightful protectorship."

His lips set grimly before he spoke again. "My lords, if the Dowager Queen cannot be persuaded to come forth with the young Duke of York, his person must be secured and removed from sanctuary."

Old Thomas Bourchier, Archbishop of Canterbury, was horrified. "You cannot do such a thing, my lord Protector! Would you violate a refuge sanctified by St. Peter himself?"

Some councillors who were lords spiritual agreed, but other churchmen of their number felt that the violation of the law of sanctuary was justified, as did all the lords temporal. Thus Richard of Gloucester's proposal was accepted.

On June 16 the council, with a body of armed men, sailed up the Thames from the Tower to Westminster. The soldiers surrounded the Abbey, while the councillors went inside. The Archbishop of Canterbury and Lord John Howard were selected to enter the abbot's quarters, where the Dowager Queen Elizabeth and the young prince were lodged.

The old archbishop used all his powers of persuasion to gain Elizabeth's consent, for the thought of force being used in the sacred place appalled him. But at first she was steadfast in her refusal.

"I say again, my Lady Queen, your son will not be harmed!" Bourchier pleaded. "He will be treated respectfully, with the most tender care!"

There was actually nothing the Dowager Queen could do, and she knew it. Putting as good a face on it as she could, she consented.

With the archbishop holding his hand, Prince Richard was taken out of the abbey and down the Thames to the Tower. There he was placed in the apartments of his brother, King Edward V.

Once young Prince Richard was safely in the Tower, all of

Richard of Gloucester's efforts were directed toward making himself King. After Hastings' execution he issued a complete account of the conspiracy which had caused it. Nevertheless, London was shocked and disturbed. Next Gloucester decided that his three prisoners in Yorkshire, who included Anthony Woodville, Earl Rivers, must be executed.

At Pontefract another chapter was added to the castle's bloody history when the three men were beheaded there.

Since the two royal brothers, Edward V and Prince Richard, had been seen practicing archery on the Tower green, they were then known to be alive. Edward V was still King and his brother next in line for the throne. Thus both were obstacles in Richard of Gloucester's path. But the duke held what he considered a trump card in the game.

Robert Stillington, Bishop of Bath and Wells, had come secretly to Gloucester with a story supposed to prove that Edward IV and Elizabeth Woodville had not been legally married. If this were true, then Edward V was not the legal King, nor his brother legal heir-apparent. And since Edward IV's brother, the Duke of Clarence, had been outlawed under a bill of attainder after his death, his children were not in line for the throne either. That left Richard, Duke of Gloucester, youngest brother of Edward IV, the true heir to the crown. There seems not to be the slightest truth in this tale of Skillington's, but it was "proof" enough for Gloucester.

When a Parliament assembled at Westminster on June 25, a parchment roll was read to the members, setting forth the "illegal" marriage of Edward IV to Elizabeth Woodville, as well as certain other even more flimsy claims by Richard, Duke of Gloucester, to the throne. Nevertheless, Parliament approved it.

The next day a vast crowd of nobles, high churchmen and citizens gathered at Baynard's Castle in the City to hear the Duke of Buckingham read the parchment scroll and call upon Gloucester to take the throne. Richard made a coy show of hesitation before accepting.

This short, sturdy man with a thick neck then rode at the head of a procession to Westminster Hall. There, in the Court of the King's Bench, he seated himself in the traditional marble chair, the King's Bench, as Justicer, the King's title as the highest judge of the realm. There he took the royal oath before the judges of the various high courts.

From Westminster Hall, Richard went first to the Abbey, where the abbot presented him with the sceptre of Edward the Confessor, then to St. Paul's, making offerings at both altars. That night he was proclaimed King Richard III of England. He was crowned in Westminster Abbey on June 6, 1483, with all the pomp of English coronations.

About three weeks later the new King set out on a progress through the kingdom. He visited Reading, Oxford and then Gloucester in the west country. Richard III then began to hear rumours of discontent in England over his seizure of the throne, and that many people wanted Edward V restored. Nevertheless, he continued his progress. He turned north to Tewkesbury and Worcester, then east to Warwick, where he spent a week in festivities. Next he set out for York by way of Coventry, Leicester, Nottingham, Doncaster and Pontefract. In York he knighted his son Edward as Prince of Wales.

The King then headed south through eastern England. Either at Lincoln, which he reached October 11, or on the way, he learned that the Duke of Buckingham had betrayed him and a rebellion was in the making.

Buckingham had not started it. What was left of the Woodville family and a number of old Lancastrian nobles in the south and southwest organized it. Sometime in September, Buckingham joined the plot. The real reason for the uprising was the rumour spreading over the land from London that Edward V and his brother were dead.

Why did Richard III's great friend Buckingham turn against him? The old chronicles tell different stories. The best evidence seems to be that the many honours bestowed on him and the heights to which he had risen went to Buckingham's head, and he decided to make a grab for the highest of them all—the throne.

The smouldering revolt burst into flame at Newbury in Berkshire, Maidstone in Kent, Guildford in Surrey, Salisbury in Wiltshire and Exeter in Devon. Meanwhile, Buckingham and a Welsh army, marching to join the rioters, crossed the border to Weobley in Herefordshire.

Meanwhile, Richard III hastened southward. At Leicester a large force joined him, and his friend John Howard, Duke of Norfolk, was in firm control of the defence of London. The King offered large rewards for the capture of the Duke of Buckingham and the other leaders of the rebellion. Then he led his army south to Coventry, resolved to drive a wedge between Buckingham and the rebels in the west and south, hurl all his force upon his old friend and destroy him.

Buckingham's army was small, and ahead of it Richard's supporters had systematically wrecked bridges, blocked roads and set ambushes in narrow passes. With that, the rebel duke's army began to melt away. Panic overcame Buckingham. He disguised himself as a countryman and galloped north into Shropshire. But he was soon run to earth and brought to the

King at Salisbury. He was quickly tried, condemned and executed in the marketplace. The rebellion then collapsed.

Peace restored, King Richard returned to London. He took revenge upon the rebel leaders in various ways, though only ten men were executed for treason. Then he began the real business of his reign.

There remained one serious trouble to haunt him. Where were Edward V and his brother, Prince Richard?

They are known as the little princes, though one was the uncrowned King Edward V. Just what happened to them has been argued for centuries, and still no one has proved the truth—who murdered them, if they were murdered, why, how, when and exactly where.

This much is known: King Edward V and Prince Richard disappeared after they were placed in the Tower. In 1674 workmen, tearing down a stone stairway in one of the several towers along the walls, discovered a wooden chest containing two skeletons in the foundations of the staircase. Today the place is known as the Bloody Tower, and the spot is pointed out by guides to a host of tourists each year.

It was believed that these were the bones of the little princes, and they were placed in an urn and enshrined in Westminster Abbey. More than two centuries later, modern science was used to determine more about the skeletons. A noted physician and an eminent dentist examined the bones in 1933. They decided the remains were those of one child between twelve and thirteen years old (Edward V was thirteen in November, 1483, presumably the year they disappeared) and another child about ten (Prince Richard's age on June 17, 1483).

For many years people believed that Richard III either had

had the two boys murdered or had done it himself. Richard had seized the throne on the most feeble of pretences, and the unrest in England that had followed was good reason for him to be rid of Edward V and his brother Richard, heir-apparent to the throne.

William Shakespeare is believed to have written his tragedy *Richard III* somewhere between 1590 and 1592. He pictured the King as a monster as black-hearted as anyone who had ever appeared on a stage. As a playwright he had the privilege of changing history to make it more dramatic, though in his historical plays he stuck quite closely to the facts. But in creating the character of Richard III he outdid himself, and it is due to this play that almost everyone came to think of Richard as a bloody-handed, ruthless murderer.

Where did Shakespeare get his information? In 1543 Sir Thomas More wrote the *History of King Richard III*. In it he described how Richard prevailed upon Sir James Tyrell to arrange the murders. Tyrell is said to have hired the ruffians who did the deed by stuffing the boys' pillows into their mouths. For much of the material in his play, Shakespeare relied upon Sir Thomas' account.

Sir Thomas More was a great and honourable statesman who was later executed for defying Henry VIII when that king abolished the Catholic Church in England. In 1935 Pope Pius XI canonized him as Saint Thomas More.

But unfortunately, More's book was written from hearsay—a supposed confession by Sir James Tyrell before he was executed for treason in 1502. From time to time after More's book was published in 1543, other writers cast doubt upon Richard's guilt. But it was not until 1768 that Horace Walpole, Earl of Oxford, a celebrated English wit and letter writer, published

Historic Doubts on the Life and Reign of Richard III, present-
ing new evidence to show that Richard was innocent, and
tearing More's account to shreds. Walpole concluded that
there was not only no proof that Richard III was responsible
for the murders, but none that they were ever committed at all.

Other writers and historians have since cast more doubt on
Richard III's guilt. Yet one thing in More's book cannot be
disputed. He tells exactly where the two boys were buried, and
that is where the bones were found. The murderers, he says,
"fetched Sir James to see them. Who, upon the sight of them,
caused these murderers to bury them at the stair-foot, meetly
deep in the ground under a great heap of stones."

True, it might have been another stairway, but that a different *two* sets of bones would be discovered at the foot of this
particular stairway is hard to believe.

Assuming that the boys were murdered, who besides Richard III would have wanted them out of the way? There were
at least two persons.

One was Henry Stafford, Duke of Buckingham. The evidence of his betrayal of Richard III and joining the rebellion
against him points to a decision to become King of England.
So he had reason to want to be rid of the two princes. And he
remained in London for a time after King Richard had started
his progress. He might have been able to get his hands on the
two boys or hire someone to do it for him.

Another possible suspect is Henry Tudor. He had good
reason to want the two boys disposed of, because Tudor was
then plotting an invasion of England to put himself on the
throne. He was far away, an exile in Brittany, yet he had
friends and agents working for his cause in England.

The strongest evidence against Richard III is that he had

already shown himself as completely ruthless in seizing the throne, and in ridding himself of those who might have taken it away from him. The bloody trail of heads in his wake proves that. About the only man who ever seriously menaced his crown whom he failed to be rid of was Henry Tudor—something Edward IV had tried to do in vain.

However, no one knows the truth. Certainly Shakespeare was unfair to Richard III. But as to whether he or someone else was responsible for the disappearance of the little princes, the reader of history must decide for himself.

XIV

Beginning of the End

Richard III was well aware that he was unpopular in England and had many enemies. He did what he could to conciliate them. The worst, of course, were the remaining Woodvilles, especially the Dowager Queen Elizabeth, still in sanctuary at Westminster Abbey with her five living daughters. The new king decided to make peace with her.

On March 1, 1484, before a great assemblage of lords and the mayor and aldermen of London, Richard swore a solemn oath that if "the daughters of Elizabeth Grey, late calling herself Queen of England" (since he had seized the throne on the pretext that her marriage to Edward IV was illegal, he used her first husband's name) would come out of their sanctuary, he would see that they were safe, were properly treated and not imprisoned and would be married to gentlemen and given proper lands and houses. He also swore to give "Dame Elizabeth Grey" a handsome income for the rest of her life.

The Dowager Queen did not then come out of sanctuary, but she did send her daughters into the world. In fact, there were strong rumours that Richard intended to find some excuse to break up his marriage to his Queen, the former Anne Neville, daughter of Warwick. She had borne him an heir to the throne, Edward, but in April, 1484, the boy prince died. Anne's marriage to Richard had not been happy; there had been no more children, and there seemed no prospect of another heir to the throne. The rumours that Richard intended to marry the Dowager Queen Elizabeth's oldest daughter, the Lady Elizabeth, increased when she appeared at a royal banquet in a robe of the same colour, material and design as Queen Anne's.

Anne saved her husband the trouble of getting rid of her by dying in March, 1485. It happened during an eclipse of the sun, and to the superstitious people of England this was an omen of dark foreboding. Richard definitely planned to marry the Lady Elizabeth, but public feeling against it was so strong that the King's advisers counselled him to forget it, and he did, issuing a public denial of any such intentions. Richard also saw to it that the widows of some of the men he had beheaded, including Anthony Woodville's wife, Lady Rivers, and the Duchess of Buckingham, were made financially secure.

The King then resolved, as had Edward IV, to get his hands on Henry Tudor, his most feared enemy. He failed in negotiations for Henry's surrender with Duke Francis of Brittany, but a little later the duke suffered fits of insanity and his chief officer, Pierre Landois, took over the reins of government. He agreed to deliver Henry to Richard in return for a military alliance against France.

Some of Henry's friends became aware of the plan. Louis XI of France had died, and a regent reigned for the boy King Charles VIII. The French Court agreed to give Henry Tudor, his uncle, Jasper Tudor, and their followers refuge, and they escaped in safety to France.

Thus, with Henry Tudor still a very real menace, Richard III strove mightily to appease his people and gain their goodwill. He got Parliament to pass a number of laws designed to relieve the common people of oppression and force the courts to deal out justice fairly. And he saw to it personally that this was done.

It did him little good, however. Some of the King's officers and advisers were bitterly hated by the people. One was Sir William Catesby, a member of the council, whom Lord Hastings had trusted, only to find that Catesby was spying on his conspiracy against the then Duke of Gloucester, now Richard III. Another was Sir Richard Ratcliffe, who had carried out the King's order to behead Anthony Woodville, Earl Rivers, and the other two prisoners at Pontefract. A third was Viscount Francis Lovell, King Richard's chamberlain.

All three were considered tyrants. One day a Welsh gentleman, William Colynbourne, having been accused of treason, fastened a rhyme to the door of St. Paul's:

> *The Cat, the Rat, and Lovell our dog*
> *Rule all England under an Hog.*

The cat was Catesby, the Rat, Ratcliffe, and "an Hog" referred to King Richard's livery of the White Boar. Colynbourne's defiance did him no good, for he was hanged, cut down while still alive and his bowels ripped out of his stomach and cast into a fire before his dying eyes. But the rhyme was repeated with glee throughout England. No, Richard III was not beloved by his subjects.

However, with an invasion of England by Henry Tudor

increasingly rumoured, Richard made lavish gifts of lands and money to noblemen who might serve and raise fighting men for him. And he announced an end forever to all "benevolences."

Nor did Richard forget the Church, whose support he needed. He founded a chapel at Middleham and a college of priests just outside the Tower. At York he provided money for a hundred priests to say masses for his soul in its great minster. And he did many other charitable acts.

All this could not stop Henry Tudor's preparations, however. Henry was a typical Welshman, calculating, cool-headed, silent, a man who kept his own counsel and had few intimate friends. Sir Francis Bacon, the great philosopher, statesman and essayist, who wrote Henry's biography, said his face was "reserved and a little like a churchman," and also remarked that ". . . he was governed by none." Bacon's description is different from Henry Tudor's appearance in a painting of him, as an older man than in 1485, that hangs in the National Portrait Gallery in London. Shrewdness, foxiness and mistrust fairly radiate from it.

This was the man who was getting ready to invade England in quest of the throne, which he claimed by rather shaky evidence of legitimate descent from King Edward III.

One of Henry's first acts to bolster his support in England took place in the cathedral of Rennes, Brittany, on Christmas morning in 1483, before his flight to France. There, in a solemn ceremony, he swore to marry Edward IV's daughter, the Lady Elizabeth, the same one Richard III had considered wedding. Thus the houses of Lancaster and the White Rose of York would be united.

One problem for Henry Tudor was that he was almost unknown in England. He had appeared just once at Court, when his uncle, Jasper Tudor, brought him to receive the blessing of his uncle, Henry VI, before both Tudors were forced into exile. Nevertheless, there were plenty of discontented men in England ready to aid him.

Henry made a wise decision—to invade England from his native Wales, where he would be able to raise a large force. The Welsh bards were already singing that the Black Bull of Anglesey (the Tudors came from the large Welsh island of Anglesey, just off the northwest coast) would defeat the White Boar, Richard III.

Henry Tudor was keeping in touch with the Stanleys. Their aid would be important because of their power in North Wales, Cheshire and Lancashire, though no doubt he was aware of their untrustworthy ways. And there were other strong figures in Wales whose help Henry counted upon.

Meanwhile, things were not going well for Richard III. He had to raise a big army, and this would cost money. He sold many of his valuable treasures, but it was not enough, and he broke his promise and resumed collecting "benevolences." And in many cases he did not know who were his friends and who his enemies. More and more nobles were arrested for treason. Worst of all, King Richard could not learn from which direction the invasion would come. He took up a position with his army at Nottingham, the most central point from which to strike in any direction at an invader.

Henry Tudor was certainly going to need all the support he could possibly get once he had landed in Wales and begun his march across England. When he sailed from Harfleur on August 1, 1485, he had only about 2,000 men aboard his ships. Yet sail he did.

XV

Bosworth Field

On August 7, 1485, Henry Tudor's small fleet of ships stood into the fine harbour of Milford Haven in Pembrokeshire, Wales. The vessels were tiny compared with modern ones, probably not unlike the little caravels in which Columbus would set out on his first voyage to the New World seven years later—towering high at the stern, with two or three masts, rigged partly with square and partly with lateen or triangular sails. The army they carried was small.

Henry Tudor was the first person to land on the sandy beach of Milford Haven. He was then a slender young man of twenty-eight, of little more than average height, with hair that the mythical King Midas might have touched to give it its golden glory, very deep-set blue eyes and high cheekbones in a rather long face with a jutting chin that proclaimed determination. He was going to need much determination and courage to carry out this invasion of England.

Henry Tudor, claiming direct descent from King Edward III of England, threw himself flat, kissed the ground and recited in Latin the beginning of Psalm 43 of the Bible: "Judge

me, O God, and plead my cause . . ." His cause, of course, was
to overthrow the Yorkish King Richard III, and put himself
on the throne as Henry VII.

As Henry had hoped, since King Richard would be more
likely to guard the southern coast of England along the English Channel against invasion, no enemy fleet had been prowl-
ing the seas off the western coast. And although Richard had
heard rumours of the approaching invasion, he apparently did
not learn of the landing for about four days. That gave Henry
Tudor precious time.

Henry had been right in his belief that Welshmen and
others might come to his aid as he marched north along the
Welsh coast, probably as far as Aberystwyth in Cardiganshire,
before swinging northeast toward Shrewsbury, England. A
number of bands of Welshmen, including a detachment from
northwest Wales and others, joined him.

King Richard had taken some precautions in case the expected invasion should come by way of Henry Tudor's native
Wales. Supplies and equipment to resist the invaders had been
gathered at several points. Henry and his army were able to
seize some of these along their route. And on August 15,
Shrewsbury, the shire town of Shropshire, proved friendly
and opened its gates to the invading army.

Meanwhile, Henry had sent messages to other possible allies.
By far the most important of these were the Stanleys, so
dominant in North Wales and in Cheshire and Lancaster in
northwest England.

Lord Thomas Stanley and his brother Sir William were the
great question marks. They had every reason to oppose the
Yorkist King. Not only were they Lancastrians, but Lord
Stanley was the third husband of Henry Tudor's mother,

Margaret Beaufort (she had first married Edmund Tudor, Earl of Richmond, Henry's father). Yet Sir William was chamberlain—a presiding royal officer—of North Wales under King Richard's rule, and there was Lord Stanley's strong support of Richard's Yorkist predecessor, Edward IV.

However, Henry Tudor had reason to believe that the Stanleys would join him with their armies of several thousand men. That would bring his strength to at least half of King Richard's mighty host. And as Henry continued his march, after having been joined beyond Shrewsbury by Sir Gilbert Talbot with about five hundred men, he met Sir William Stanley at Stafford and held a conference with him. What was said and promised at that meeting, no one knows with certainty.

From Stafford, Henry's army turned southeast until it reached the thriving town of Lichfield. The city opened its gates and received him. From there he moved on to the hamlet of Tamworth. Henry and his men were now in the Midlands.

Henry left his camp for a short time and went on to the little village of Atherstone. There he met and held a conference with both the Stanleys. The result could not have raised his hopes much, for apparently all that came of it was a rather vague promise that they and their armies would give Henry support when the right moment arrived.

That moment might never come. The two noblemen, especially Lord Stanley, had a powerful reason not to make a definite promise of aid. It was fear for the safety of Lord Stanley's son, Lord George Strange.

On August 16, 1485, King Richard III marched his army out of the marketplace of Nottingham and through a gate in the city's walls. He was mounted on a superb white charger.

On top of the helmet that was a part of his polished steel armour perched a golden circlet, a crown of sorts, so that all might know that here rode Richard III, King of England.

He was a bad man to have for an enemy, this dark-haired king with the ruthless, piercing eyes that seemed to bore straight through the onlookers. At times Richard's speech and manners were gentle, but it is said that two signs warned those who knew him not to irritate him further if they had already done so. When his hand played with the dagger at his side, lifting it partly out of its sheath and dropping it back again, and when he nibbled at his lower lip—these were danger signals.

Richard III had been for some time with his Court at Nottingham Castle, of which he was fond. The moment he learned of Henry Tudor's landing he dispatched couriers throughout the kingdom to summon the nobles he could rely upon to aid him with the forces of fighting men they maintained. Among them were the Stanleys, and they had marched in the general direction of the rendezvous at Leicester.

Richard remained at Nottingham until a large force had gathered there. Then, deciding he could wait no longer for further reinforcements, he marched about twenty-five miles south to Leicester. It was a scene of pomp and splendour. Trumpets blared and colour was rampant. Many men wore Richard's livery of the White Boar on their sleeves or backs, while the livery of others was the White Rose of Yorkshire or that of the lord they served. There were many pennons and standards too, banners of brilliant hue and varied designs.

The Yorkist army was separated into two divisions, each marching five abreast, with the army's baggage following the first division. Then came the King and finally the second division. The foot soldiers wore coats of leather with chain mail fastened beneath it. The mounted men rode along the wings of the column near the centre. Those of Richard's cavalry known as cuirassiers wore only breast and back armour. Other horsemen and the mounted leaders were almost fully encased in armour, and their steeds were armoured too.

Although Richard's "scurriers" (scouts) had brought word that his army was far superior in numbers to that of Henry Tudor, the King was a little uneasy, for the Stanleys had not yet joined him as he had commanded. Nevertheless, one thing in that connection heartened him.

For some months he had been suspicious of the Stanleys' loyalty. Early in that year of 1485 Lord Stanley, who was at the Court, had asked leave to go to Lancashire and visit his family. When he did not return after several months, Richard had commanded him either to come in person to the Court or send his son and heir, Lord Strange, in his place. Lord Stanley, not daring to disobey, had sent Lord Strange to the Court at Nottingham.

This was Richard III's ace in the game which was about to begin. He felt sure that with Lord Strange as his hostage, the young nobleman's life would not be sacrificed by his father and uncle. They knew that the King would not hesitate a moment to execute him if the Stanleys joined Henry Tudor. And in spite of Richard's larger army, the Stanleys might well decide the outcome of this all-important battle by what they did.

Again with much magnificence, Richard and his army moved out of Leicester on Sunday, August 21. More men had joined him, making an army estimated at between 8,000 and 10,000 men. With Lord Strange as additional security, King Richard was now confident.

He headed straight toward the hamlet of Market Bosworth, about twelve miles away, and half a dozen from Henry Tudor's army, now at Atherstone, a little to the southwest. The Yorkist army camped near Sutton Cheney, another hamlet, in rolling country that made it possible to see the flatter lands just beyond.

That same night Henry Tudor's army camped on a plain called the White Moors, a little over two miles southwest of Sutton Cheney. Between him and the enemy were a little rill called Sence Brook, then a field which was partly marsh, and finally a rise of ground known as Ambien Hill.

Bosworth Field, as it is called, can be seen today, though it is tucked away, almost unmarked, in one of the most rural parts of England, a dozen miles from the city of Leicester. This scene of one of the most important battles ever fought on English soil is not much changed from the way it must have looked five centuries ago, except for a wooded area that now covers part of it. The little Sence still runs through the cornfields and the gentle hum of insects can still be heard in the stillness of a warm August morning. The marsh is pretty well dried up, though a little boggy in spots. Ambien Hill has several farmhouses that were not there in 1485, but otherwise it looks much the same.

The hill was a key point, since its elevation would give the army occupying it an advantage. By dawn on August 22, Richard's scouts had occupied it, and the King then marched there with all speed from Sutton Cheney. John Howard, Duke of Norfolk, led the Yorkist army's van. Close behind him was the King with the main body, followed by Henry Percy, Earl of Northumberland, with the rear guard.

Where were the Stanleys? That mystery was solved when

the Yorkist army deployed for battle on Ambien Hill. King Richard and his chiefs could see them plainly from the hilltop. Lord Stanley's men were gathered to the southeast, some distance away. In the opposite direction, to the northwest, was Sir William's force. It was also at a distance, but if an old poem about the battle is to be believed, they were highly visible, for it says that Sir William's men wore red coats emblazoned with his livery, a hart's head.

Yet there was no indication of what the Stanleys intended to do. Richard beckoned to a courier. "Haste to Lord Stanley's camp with my command that he join me at once. Say that if he fail me his son will be instantly beheaded."

The courier was off like an arrow, and as soon back. "Lord Stanley replies to your Grace," he reported, "that he will not join you now. As for your Grace's promise to behead Lord Strange, he replies that he has other sons."

The King's face flamed with fury. "Behead Lord Strange!" he fairly screamed.

A dozen hands seized the young nobleman. But for some reason it appears that others of the King's leaders interfered. Perhaps this was Richard's first inkling that there might be treachery against him if the battle did not go well for the Yorkists, that these dissenters feared Henry Tudor's vengeance if Lord Strange were executed. They seem to have managed to induce Richard to countermand the order, perhaps saying: better a king who might escape with his life to fight another day than a dead one, if the battle went against him.

This the Stanleys could not know, of course, yet they still made no move toward either side. Nevertheless, Lord Stanley's refusal and the actions of his own subordinates must have disturbed the King. One of the chroniclers of the period declares that Richard had spent a restless night, beset by hideous night-mares. Richard III trusted few men, being himself a man not to be trusted, and these events were indications that some among his leaders might desert him if it seemed to their advantage.

As for Henry Tudor, his efforts to find out what the Stanleys would do were equally fruitless. He too sent an appeal to Lord Stanley to join him. The reply was vague. Henry, the Lord said, should set his own force in order and in time he would be aided. "In time" did not please the Lancastrian commander, whom a chronicler describes as "no little vexed" and "somewhat appalled."

However, there was nothing to do but to go ahead. Henry ordered his army formed for attack. To John de Vere, Earl of Oxford, he said, "Lead the archers at the head of the advance." And to Sir Gilbert Talbot, with his five hundred men, he said: "Take the right of the line to defend the archers." Henry gave command of the left side to Sir John Savage, while he himself followed with a troop of horsemen.

The sight of Richard's army drawn up on the hill in the distance, twice the size of his own, must have been discouraging to Henry as he gave the order to advance. He might have felt better if he had known that many a man in that enemy host did not have the heart for a real fight in support of Richard III. These men were on the King's side only because they expected him to win. They had no real loyalty to him.

With a great blast of trumpets, Henry Tudor's army moved forward across the fields between the White Moors and Ambien Hill. Although no records mention it, both sides probably had some small, crude cannon. But the chief use of artillery then was to batter down the walls of castles and fortresses during sieges. While both sides would have brought their cannon into action as the battle began, they were probably ineffective.

It appears that Henry's scurriers had not warned him of the marsh in his path. When his advance force, having crossed Sence Brook, reached it they had to wheel sharply to the left to avoid it, and this caused some confusion in the ranks. Richard, watching from the hilltop, must have been tempted to take advantage of this and send the Duke of Norfolk, with the left wing, down the hill in a charge, but he decided it was better to hold his ground.

As Henry Tudor's army approached closer to Ambien Hill, the battle began with a furious interchange by the bowmen of both sides. The steel-tipped arrows did terrible execution, but the bowmen could carry only so many of them, and as had happened before in the Wars of the Roses, soon this ammunition began to run short on both sides.

As the shower of arrows slackened, both sides waited for the other to make the next move. Meanwhile, both the Stanleys hovered in the background, making no advance to join either side.

At last, however, Henry Tudor's army advanced up the hill toward the Yorkist left wing. The Duke of Norfolk's men moved down and met them at about the middle of Ambien Hill's southward slope. The mainstays of both armies then clashed in savage combat—the billmen with their terrible bills and the cavalry with their sharp, gleaming swords.

The opposing armies were now locked in a bloody, hand-to-hand death struggle. It went on for about an hour, with neither side gaining a real advantage. John de Vere, Earl of Oxford, leading Henry Tudor's Lancastrian advance, while

Tudor himself remained to the rear with the main body, was gaining ground, but he saw that too rapid movement ahead could put him in peril of being surrounded before the main army came up.

"Plant the standards here," Oxford ordered the flag bearers. Then he shouted: "Let no man advance more than ten feet beyond these standards!"

Gradually, Henry Tudor and the main army came up and into action, engaging King Richard's centre division. The King, watching the Stanleys, saw them moving at last. Usually pale, his face grew ashen, for it seemed that they were heading to join Henry Tudor.

If the King did not realize then that his doom was approaching, he must have when he looked at his army's right wing. There the Earl of Northumberland was doing nothing at all. Perhaps Richard smelled treason, sensing that the earl was waiting to see what the Stanleys would do before moving himself.

But there could no longer be any doubt about the Stanleys in Richard's despairing mind. They were in action now. Sir William Stanley and his men had moved in from the north-west to attack the King's own centre; Lord Stanley from the southeast against Norfolk.

One of the King's couriers pleaded, "Fly, your Grace! All is lost!"

Richard's answer, if he gave one, was probably a snarl of refusal. In the hot August morning he slaked his thirst at a little spring (it is still there), leaped to his charger's back, gathered his subordinates about him and charged recklessly down the hill, straight into the thick of the battle, where Henry Tudor's standard fluttered in the breeze.

It was shortly after this moment, William Shakespeare wrote in his tragedy *Richard III,* that the King shouted in anguish: "A horse! A horse! My kingdom for a horse!" The great playwright and poet may have invented the lines; though he knew his history well, reliable historians say that while Richard's horse was slain in these last moments of the battle, another had been brought to him.

The king fought like a demon to the very last, beset on every side by savage enemies. He cleft off the head of Henry Tudor's gigantic standard bearer with one stroke of his sword. Then he seized Henry's standard, a red dragon on a green and white background, an ancient Welsh device of his ancestors, and hurled it to the ground. Richard's object in this final, hopeless struggle was to get at Henry.

At last a blow struck him down. His foes swarmed in on him, hacking and stabbing. In his last breath he gasped two words: "Treason! Treason!"

In the melee someone had struck the golden crown from his head. King Richard's army was now in full flight from Bosworth Field. A plundering Lancastrian spied the crown, seized it and hid it in a thorn bush, but it was soon discovered. When the victorious army had moved a short distance southward to a little hill that became known as Crown Hill, Lord Stanley brought the battered circlet up, placed it on Henry Tudor's head and hailed him as King Henry VII.

Indeed, as the dying Richard had cried, treason had set the crown on Henry's head. Treason by the Stanleys, who had given their loyalty to Richard when his power was secure. Treason by Henry Percy, Earl of Northumberland, who had played the dead King false. He profited richly from it, for instead of being imprisoned or executed as were two captured

Yorkist leaders, he was immediately received into the favour of Henry VII.

There are no reliable figures as to the casualties on either side. Richard had lost an estimated thousand men, including the Duke of Norfolk and other noblemen. Henry Tudor's losses were far less, probably only about a hundred, with only one of high rank killed, the standard bearer, Sir William Brandon.

Bosworth Field was not the greatest battle of the Wars of the Roses if numbers of men engaged are considered; nor was it the bloodiest in losses. And strangely, of the thirteen principal battles fought in the thirty-year struggle, the Yorkists won nine, the Lancastrians only four. But the side that wins the final battle triumphs, and at Bosworth Field it was Lancaster.

This was the end and the beginning. It was the end of thirty years of off-again-on-again, brutal, bloody war, of endless intrigues and treachery and the strife between Lancaster and York. And by keeping his promise to marry Lady Elizabeth, daughter of the Yorkist King Edward IV, Henry Tudor united the two great houses and began a new dynasty, the Tudors.

It was the start of a golden era. The Tudor kings and queens included some of England's greatest rulers. Wicked and cruel some were, but they put England on the road to great accomplishments that would reach their height in the nineteenth century, when Britain became the greatest and most powerful empire in the world.

Suggested Further Readings

Of the books on the history of the Wars of the Roses that should easily be obtained in libraries, three stand out.

The first is *Bosworth Field,* by A. L. Rowse, published by Macmillan & Co. in 1966. Mr. Rowse, a distinguished English historian and noted authority on Shakespeare, has written many books, chiefly on English history. He writes simply, interestingly and accurately, and this book is easy to read and understand, and is one of the best full accounts of the Wars of the Roses for the reader who does not want too much detailed background on an extremely complicated subject.

Next come two volumes by an American college professor, Paul Murray Kendall. They are *Richard the Third* and *Warwick the Kingmaker,* both published by Allen & Unwin, the first in 1955 and the second in 1957. Both are brilliant, well written, detailed accounts. In *Richard the Third,* Mr. Kendall discusses at length the great controversy over whether Richard was responsible for the deaths of the "little princes."

The best-known authority on the Wars of the Roses is James H. Ramsey, whose *Lancaster and York* was published in Eng-

land by the Clarendon Press in 1892 and may be obtainable
in some libraries. In two large volumes, Mr. Ramsey covered
every incident connected with the Wars of the Roses and the
government of England in the fifteenth century, starting long
before the wars themselves began. These are volumes for those
who want to delve deeply into the entire subject or certain
parts of it.

For an easily readable account of life in England in the
fifteenth century, written for young people, the first volume of
Marjorie and C. H. B. Quennell's four-volume *A History of
Everyday Things in England,* published in London by B. T.
Batsford in 1950, is one of the best and most interesting.

Bibliography

Burne, Alfred H. *The Battlefields of England*. London: Methuen & Co., Ltd., 1950.

Christie, Mabel E. *Henry VI*. London: Constable & Co., Ltd., 1922.

Clair, Colin. *A Brief History of Westminster Abbey*. Watford, Hertfordshire: Bruce & Cawthorn, Ltd. (no date).

Ehrlich, Blake. *London on the Thames*. Boston: Little, Brown & Co., 1966.

Fisher, Graham (editor). *Historic Britain*. Watford, Hertfordshire: Oldham (Watford) Ltd. (no date, recent).

Fry, Plantagenet Somerset. *Rulers of Britain*. London: Paul Hamlyn, 1967.

Gairdner, James. *History of the Life and Reign of Richard the Third*. Cambridge, England: University Press, 1898.

Hall, Edward. *Hall's Chronicle*. London: Printed for J. Johnson, F. C. and J. Rivington, T. Payne, Wilkie and Robinson, Longman, Hurst, Rees and Orme, Cadell and Davies, and J. Newman, 1809, collated with the edition of 1548 and 1550.

Hanson, Michael. *2000 Years of London*. London: Country Life, 1967.

Howgego, J. L. *The City of London Through Artists' Eyes.* New York: Walker & Co., 1969.

Hill, Georgiana. *A History of English Dress.* New York: G. P. Putnam's Sons, 1893.

Hutton, William. *The Battle of Bosworth Field.* London: Nichols, Son, and Bentley, 1813.

Joseph, Richard. *Your Trip to Britain.* Garden City: Doubleday & Co., 1954.

Kendall, Paul Murray. *Richard the Third.* New York: W. W. Norton & Co., 1956.

————. *Richard III, The Great Debate.* New York: W. W. Norton & Co., 1965.

————. *Warwick the Kingmaker.* New York: W. W. Norton & Co., 1957.

Leary, Frances. *The Golden Longing.* New York: Chas. Scribner's Sons, 1959.

Magoffin, Ralph V. D., and Duncalf, Frederic. *Ancient and Medieval History.* Morristown, N. J.: Silver Burdett Co., 1957.

Marston, E. W. *The Book of the Village.* London: Phoenix House, 1962.

Meyrick, Dr. (drawings), and Skelton, Joseph. *Engraved Illustrations of Ancient Arms and Armour.* Oxford: Joseph Skelton (no date).

More, Thomas (J. Rawson, editor). *The Historie of Kyng Richard the Thirde.* Cambridge: University Press, 1883 (first published 1557).

Oman, Charles W. *Warwick the Kingmaker.* London: Macmillan & Co., 1891.

Quennell, Marjorie and C. H. B. *A History of Everyday Things in England.* London: B. T. Batsford Ltd., 1950.

Ramsey, James H. *Lancaster and York.* Oxford: Clarendon Press, 1892.

Rowse, A. L. *Bosworth Field.* London: Macmillan, 1966.

Scofield, Cora L. *The Life and Reign of Edward the Fourth.* London: Longmans, Green & Co., 1923.

Simons, Eric N. *The Reign of Edward IV.* London: Frederick Muller, Ltd., 1966.

Smith, Goldwin. *A History of England.* New York: Chas. Scribner's Sons, 1966.

Smith, Lacey Baldwin. "The Wars of the Roses." Horizon, Winter, 1969, Vol. XI, No. 1.

Strutt, Joseph. *Honda Angel-cynnan, or a Compleat View of the Manners, Customs, Habits &c. of the Inhabitants of England.* London: T. Jones, 1774.

The Tower of London. London: Her Majesty's Stationary Office, 1967.

Traill, H. D., and Mann, J. S. (editors). *Social England.* London: Cassell & Co., Ltd., 1909.

Treharne, R. F., and Fullard, Harold (editors). *Muir's New School Atlas of Universal History.* New York: Barnes & Noble, 1961.

Trevelyan, G. M. *Illustrated English Social History.* London: Longmans, Green & Co., 1950.

Vergil, Polydore. *Three Books of Polydore Vergil's History, Comprising the Reigns of Henry VI, Edward IV and Richard III.* London: Printed for the Camden Society by John Bowyer. Nichols & Son, 1944.

Wallace Collection Catalogues—European Arms and Armour. London: William Clowes & Sons, Ltd., 1962.

Walpole, Horace. *Historic Doubts on the Life of King Richard the Third.* London: J. Dodsley, 1768.

Index